Licensure in Professional Psychology

Licensure in Professional Psychology

PREPARATORY TECHNIQUES

Tony D. Crespi, Ed.D.

Taylor & Francis
Publishers since 1798

USA	Publishing Office:	Taylor & Francis 1101 Vermont Avenue, N.W., Suite 200 Washington, DC 20005-3521 Tel: (202) 289-2174 Fax: (202) 289-3665
	Distribution Center:	Taylor & Francis 1900 Frost Road, Suite 101 Bristol, PA 19007-1598 Tel: (215) 785-5800 Fax: (215) 785-5515
UK		Taylor & Francis Ltd. 4 John St. London WC1N 2ET Tel: 071 405 2237 Fax: 071 831 2035

LICENSURE IN PROFESSIONAL PSYCHOLOGY: Preparatory Techniques

1 2 3 4 5 6 7 8 9 0   B R B R   9 8 7 6 5 4

This book was set in Trump Medieval by TAPSCO, Inc. The editors were Jack Neal and Merrie L. Kaye. The production supervisor was Peggy M. Rote. Cover design by Michelle Fleitz. Printing and binding by Braun-Brumfield, Inc.

A CIP catalog record for this book is available from the British Library.

♾ The paper in this publication meets the requirements of the ANSI Standard Z39.48-1984 (Permanence of Paper)

Library of Congress Cataloging-in-Publication Data

Crespi, Tony D.
  Licensure in professional psychology: preparatory techniques / Tony D. Crespi.
    p.   cm.
  Includes index.

  1. Psychologists—United States—Examinations.   2. Psychologists—Licenses—United States.   3. Psychologists—Certification—United States.   I. Title.
BF80.8.C74   1994
150´.76—dc20   94-14145
ISBN 1-56032-310-8   CIP

For Allen E. Ivey, a licensed psychologist, distinguished professor, author, and friend. A Diplomate of the American Board of Professional Psychologists and a two-time Fulbright Scholar who earned his doctoral degree from Harvard University, Dr. Ivey's unwavering commitment to his profession and his dedication to linking theory and practice serves as a model of excellence for all psychologists. I know of no individual who more clearly embodies the highest ideals of our profession—and of humanity. If this work can help emerging psychologists reach their goals and refine their knowledge, then perhaps I have captured, in a small way, something of the spirit and legacy that Allen E. Ivey personifies and cultivates.

Contents

Foreword

You are about to embark on one of the most important professional journeys of psychology—that of obtaining state licensure. Licensure helps you to demonstrate to others in a very concrete manner that you have mastered the important content of your field. Licensure is one of the foundations on which a truly professional practice can be built.

Psychology is an immense field. When I began my work as a psychologist in 1957, I had taken virtually all of the courses that my program offered. I was able to keep pace with the journals and key books important to my work. I prided myself on my awareness of new trends in practice and in research during my early professional life. However, over the years, psychology and its journals and books have grown faster than my ability to read. I find it increasingly difficult to maintain mastery of the field and realize that I must accept the fact that I can no longer still know all the critical details.

Armed with the above knowledge, I have a particular empathy for you who are about to take the professional licensing examination. Although more courses taught at a far more sophisticated level have been made available to you than I was offered as a graduate student, you simply can't "know it all." Yet, this is approximately what the licensure examination asks you to do.

You will find that this book, *Licensure in Professional Psychology: Preparatory Techniques*, will help you to organize your approach to studying for licensure and will also facilitate your effective performance on the examination. The systematic techniques presented by Tony Crespi will enable you to constitute a plan of study, review your performance periodically, and establish exactly what needs to be done to enhance your performance. I wish I had had the benefit of this book when I took similar examinations.

When we pass an examination, we sometimes think we know it all. In this case, a very difficult and strenuous test will have been endured and mastered with honor. Enjoy your success, but be aware that psychology is a field which is rapidly expanding. Prepare yourself for a lifetime of study and growth or face almost immediate obsolescence and irrelevance. Passing the examination is but an opening to further professional development and learning.

Those of us who fail the examination need not be discouraged. Many now famous psychologists did not meet the rigors of this test the first time. Avoid letting a test define who you are as a professional. There are more important issues of competence such as your ability to relate with and help another human or to conduct meaningful research. Being able to pass an examination on ethics does not make one ethical.

If you have difficulty with examinations or have failed an earlier try, this book will be invaluable in your preparation. I am especially impressed by the comprehensive approach to planning which Crespi presents. It is easy to become overwhelmed by the task of preparing for licensure. Crespi shows how to manage the important steps toward a successful score on the examination.

Once you have mastered the examination, you can open your mind to new learnings and options. Psychology will never stand still—it will always challenge you. Whether you choose continuing education courses to maintain your licensure, reading and studying on your own, or taking one of the American Board of Professional Psychology specialty examinations, you can look forward to life in a profession which gives you constant challenge.

Today's world and psychology are very different from what I encountered in the late 1950's. As I look at Tony Crespi's important presentation on licensure, I can't help but ask myself the questions, "Would I do it again? Would I still undertake the study of psychology as a career?" The field is more complex and difficult and the clients seemingly more challenging, but I would become a psychologist again without a doubt. No field is more intellectually interesting, no field offers a larger opportunity for satisfaction in helping, and no field could offer more challenge for personal and professional growth.

Welcome to professional psychology. You are now part of its growth and development for the future. And good luck on that examination!

Allen E. Ivey, Ed.D., A.B.P.P.

Distinguished University Professor
School and Counseling Psychology Program
University of Massachusetts, Amherst

Preface

Professional psychologists typically devote a significant portion of their lives to training for professional practice. Yet, the completion of four years of undergraduate education, as well as the requisite four to five years of graduate or professional school training, while culminating in a doctoral degree, is insufficient for the regulatory requirements for independent practice. In point of fact, preparation remains abridged until the compulsory post-doctoral requirements and state and national examinations are successfully completed.

In many professions, there are key hurdles that must be faced before one is awarded the right to independent professional practice. For psychologists, licensure is one such challenge: a critical credential for those pursuing autonomous professional careers. Although the requirement of licensure (or certification) for psychologists is well-entrenched, a concerted interest in preparatory practices for psychologists pursuing such credentials has remained a less-than-prominent source of scholarly interest. The reasons for this lack of interest are many-faceted and include the regulatory requirement that mandates post-doctoral training before license eligibility (thereby distancing licensing and doctoral education). However, times are changing, and the overall importance of licensure to psychologists is of growing significance.

Although there are exceptions, most psychologists entering practice today (and we can expect this to be true tomorrow, as well), whether in private practice or in medical centers, child guidance clinics, psychiatric hospitals, correctional facilities, community counseling centers, or neuropsychological rehabilitation programs, are required to secure state licensing—typically from a branch of the state department of health services. In short, although not the only ingredient nor necessarily the most important ingredient for professional success, licensure is a key credential for those whose interests involve the professional practice of psychology.

Although it may seem ironic that licensure, even a decade ago, carried little of the import noted today, professional psychologists actually have a strong and established association with licensure boards. This relationship dates back to the 1940s, when Connecticut (in 1945) and Kentucky (in 1948) enacted laws to govern practice. Today, all 50 states and Puerto Rico and the District of Columbia have laws regulating the practice of psychology. Professional psychologists today have compelling reasons to seek licensure and to enjoy the advantages that such credentials afford. Of course, some graduates may not demonstrate an interest in licensure, possibly pursuing interests in such areas as hospital administration or academic research. However, most graduates of programs involving the differing areas of professional psychology (such as clinical psychology, school psychology, and counseling psychology) will seek licensure. Moreover, with an increasing number of graduates interested in pursuing direct-service careers, one may speculate that the procurement of state licensure will increasingly become a requisite for practice. One might surmise, even, that licensure in professional psychology eventually may become as important to psychology as licensure is to medicine—if indeed this already has not begun to transpire.

Such points well in hand, it is helpful to understand that the professional examinations for licensure in psychology, by and large, pose a tremendous challenge for most candidates, testing a breadth and range of knowledge that can sometimes seem overwhelming to even the most highly trained candidate.

For those pursuing licensure, it should be understood that the intention of this work is to provide readers with an armamentarium of strategies designed to enhance the probability of successfully accomplishing the goal of licensure. Although clearly it is the intention of licensing laws to protect the public from incompetent or inferior practitioners, licensure can also have the untoward effect of actually limiting the number of competent and qualified practitioners by inadvertently blocking otherwise competent professionals who may not successfully complete the examination process because of examination and/or study weaknesses. Fortunately, a well-organized study plan can help minimize this possibility.

When pursuing licensure, candidates can profit from a thorough and consolidated study model. In fact, readers should understand that the purpose of this work, overall, is to provide a useful reference for those interested in preparation strategies for the national licensing examination. Likewise, these strategies can also be useful for those pursuing specialty certifications.

Still, no single work can substitute for the years of academic and professional training required of professional psychologists. To the contrary, those who successfully achieve licensure must integrate and extract information from a wide array of topical areas. It is hoped that the techniques and strategies in this work can be brought to bear on the imposing professional preparatory challenges, providing key designs around which candidates for licensure can organize comprehensive preparatory study programs.

In this book, we will analyze and review various components of preparation and study useful for licensing candidates. Simply put, the more candidates know about the ingredients necessary for success on the psychology licensing examination, the better prepared they will be. Unfortunately, the licensing process needlessly frustrates too many candidates. On the other hand, for most graduates who come from sound and rigorous programs, licensure is a realistic goal when approached with a well-designed and comprehensive preparatory study program.

In considering the wide scope of subjects that are scrutinized through the examination process, no academic wizardry is necessary to understand the rationale for a well-designed, comprehensive, preparatory program of study. Furthermore, most applicants understand that licensure in psychology requires commitment. Those who attain licensing, by and large, approach the examination with a committed mindset. Here again, this is one intention of this book, as it is designed to help provide information on study strategies and test taking approaches useful for candidates for licensure. Also, practical advice is offered on how to design a study program, how to meld a study plan with conflicting real-world commitments, and how to set priorities and refine strategies that can be used while preparing for the national examination.

Fortunately, as professional examinations go, licensure is, in fact, less grueling than the requirements faced during the preparation of most doctoral dissertations. This is an important and useful corollary. Preparation for licensing in professional psychology requires a commitment—a dedication and perseverance—similar to that which most doctoral students made while completing their comprehensive examinations and doctoral dissertations. Some candidates, perhaps, will not have completed a doctoral dissertation, and this metaphor will be lacking for these candidates. Also, there are applicants, unfortunately, who may have found the preparation of a dissertation somewhat agonizing. Still, all candidates have completed certain rigorous training programs and have secured scholarly credentials evident of considerable perseverance and commitment.

A word of caution for those professionals who may consider foregoing the quest for licensure: there is a compelling body of knowledge supporting the supposition that licensure will grow in importance. Notably, psychologists have made significant strides over the past decade in achieving new rights and responsibilities as health care providers. But, while exciting, such advances greatly broaden the responsibilities felt by psychologists, and enhance the public's desire for strict regulatory controls on practice. Most likely, as the profession continues to develop, the regulatory requirements will not lessen. In fact, it is conceivable that the requirements for licensure as a psychologist could be further elevated.

The only question, then, for those interested in the professional practice of psychology, is how and when to properly prepare.

Tony D. Crespi, Ed.D.

Licensed Psychologist

Acknowledgments

The present volume reflects my long-standing interest in professional credentialing, which began in the 1970s and continues through the present. On a personal level, the critical importance of licensure and certification first became poignantly clear to me when I became aware of the fact, while pursuing my master's degree, that I would need to temporarily postpone the pursuit of a doctoral degree. Suddenly faced with the need and desire to secure professional employment, I experienced a deepening sense of apprehension given that I lacked any regulatory certifications.

Fortuitously, I was assisted during this time, and later as I completed my doctorate and post-doctorate residency, by several highly knowledgeable individuals who helped broaden my understanding of the regulatory processes that underlie certification and licensure in the mental health professions.

These individuals represent a range of psychological specialties, including clinical psychology, school psychology, and counseling psychology. Several also possess specialty interests involving areas such as health psychology, family psychology, and child psychology. As such, the breadth of influence that I received and that touches this work is multifaceted and reflects the diverse opportunities that many licensed psychologists cultivate during a career. More to the point, I have endeavored to develop a preparatory text useful to psychologists who are trained in differing specialties and have made the decision to pursue licensure.

I extend my deepest respect and appreciation to the following individuals: Jerrold T. Hanson, Ena Vazquez-Nuttall, Jay M. Cudrin, Earl S. Patterson, Melinda A. Hennen, Ronald M. Sabatelli, and Allen E. Ivey. Further, I also acknowledge the important contributions of Cheryl S. Crespi and Hope L. Pinkerton. All told, each of these individuals in a compendium of different ways has helped me to realize my own goals and has encouraged my involvements and activities as a psychologist, researcher, and author.

In my own professional development, I remain indebted to Jerrold T. Hanson, currently dean of the graduate school at Peru State College at Peru, Nebraska, who initially stimulated my interest in the credentialing process. A skillful educator and clinician who earned his doctoral degree from the University of Colorado at Boulder, Dr. Hanson unselfishly offered critical direction that enabled me to effectively pursue certification and employment in the 1970s, following my completion of a master's degree. Moreover, he helped to deepen my appreciation for the statutory processes that underlie certification and licensure as a whole. His wise guidance helped establish the initial foundation of interest that eventually led to the development of this book.

Later, while pursuing my doctoral degree at the University of Massachusetts at Amherst in the early 1980s, I had the great pleasure to work closely with Ena Vazquez-Nuttall, a psychologist who earned her doctorate at Boston University and who currently combines the roles of clinician, educator, and consultant. She is an active member of the American Psychological Association's division of counseling psychology and is a former board member of the National School Psychology Certification Board. Dr. Vazquez-Nuttall enthusiastically encouraged the pursuit of my many interests and, equally important, she served as a mainstay throughout my doctoral program. Her uncompromising support of my divergent interests, and her background and endorsement as I actively pursued my training, will always be remembered.

Aside from the scholarly and academic interests in training and licensure that I refined during these periods, my own personal interest in licensure was further stimulated through my continuing association with Jay M. Cudrin, a clinical psychologist who earned his doctorate from the University of North Carolina at Chapel Hill and the individual who, without qualification, provided invaluable clinical guidance and supervision throughout much of my training. An eloquent and soft-spoken practitioner with more than 20 years of inpatient experience, Dr. Cudrin's continuing interest in such diverse areas as alcohol and drug abuse treatment, child and family therapy, and psychological assessment provided unending stimulation as we refined and expanded my clinical skills. Equally important, if not more so, was his sincere interest in my professional development and in helping me identify and strengthen my scholarly and professional skills. Objectively, I suppose such dedication should be assumed in a clinical supervisor. Clearly, though, the qualities that set Dr. Cudrin above the crowd were his sincerity, his characteristic intellectual curiosity, and his commitment to providing the finest clinical supervision that he could muster. No words can convey the deep respect and admiration I feel toward this individual. He is more than a gifted psychologist; he has been a wonderful colleague and friend.

Also supportive while I studied for the Examination for Professional Practice in Psychology was Earl S. Patterson, M.D., F.A.P.A., a psychiatrist in private practice in Meriden, Connecticut. At different times, he provided invaluable suggestions and emotional support. Moreover, it has become obvious to me that his support served as a professional anchor that I found unusually helpful, first while I pursued my study program culminating in licensure and, more recently, as I worked on the development of this book. A loyal and strong advocate who believes deeply in the contributions of professional psychologists, Dr. Patterson is a model of excellence for all health care providers.

More recently, two new friends and colleagues have exerted a profound influence on my professional development. Melinda A. Hennen, a licensed psychologist, certified marriage and family therapist, and nationally certified school psychologist in private practice in New Haven, Connecticut, has been a friend and confidante as I have expanded my research and writing. An insightful clinician who received her doctorate from the University of Georgia, Dr. Hennen is an exemplary psychologist who continually pursues learning, despite the attainment of stellar credentials. Her commitment to the welfare of her clients, and her expressions of support for my scholarly abilities served as a wellspring of encouragement during the development of the first draft of this work. She is an outstanding clinician who serves as a model of excellence for those who intend to develop an autonomous private practice.

Ronald M. Sabatelli, a professor of family studies at the University of Connecticut at Storrs, where he earned his doctorate, has been a strong academic and scholarly supporter since I first met him in 1991. His strong endorsement and displays of confidence served as a springboard as I researched this work. Dr. Sabatelli is a gifted educator, researcher, and scholar whose sincere interest and efforts helped me explore new conceptual interests.

Also fundamental to a study and preparation program for licensure and to the preparation of a work such as this one is a familial support system. It would not have been possible to achieve my objectives without the aid of a number of individuals who are deeply involved in my life. The support I received from my wife and partner, Cheryl S. Crespi, has been especially important. Although I have learned that there are inevitable disappointments, unforeseen challenges, and unexpected difficulties in life, the support and love that family can provide truly make life's hardships pale. I know I am fortunate to share my life and my interests with Cheryl.

Throughout my professional career and, in fact, as long as I can remember, my mother, Hope L. Pinkerton, has been an unflinching supporter of my professional objectives and a compelling role model for those who view licensure and certification as important components of a lifelong commitment to professional development. My mother is a retired speech pathologist who devoted a long and rich career to the communicative needs of young children. Her unwavering belief in her own continuing education—an activity she has continued during retirement—served as a powerful role model throughout my early development. Indeed, I have many warm memories of times she enthusiastically listened, often during long-distance telephone conversations between Arizona and Connecticut, while I shared my ideas about developing this book. She is a staunch supporter of the highest professional standards for all health care providers, and often has shared or suggested some insight on professional development and professional licensure that stimulated new thinking. If the goal of licensure for health care providers is to ensure professionals who will offer only the highest standards of service, my mother certainly exemplified that quality during her many years of service as a licensed health care provider in speech-language pathology. I wish all professionals were so dedicated.

My continuing association with Allen E. Ivey, a distinguished professor and a Diplomate in counseling psychology of the American Board of Professional Psychology, has been especially important to my understanding of the legislative processes regarding licensure. Dr. Ivey was my advisor and dissertation chairman while I pursued my doctorate at the University of Massachusetts at Amherst, and he has been a nucleus of support and encouragement during my professional development.

The published articles and books of Dr. Ivey have been read throughout the world. They have been translated into numerous foreign languages, including Dutch, French, German, Japanese, Danish, and Swedish. As a consultant and university trainer, he has spoken at many universities, including Stanford, Columbia, Cornell, the University of Puerto Rico, the University of Florida, Bucknell University, the University of Hawaii, the University of Lund in Sweden, and Flinders University in Australia. Even with all these successes, his warmth, his unselfish devotion to his students, and the richness of his relationships with his friends and his family stand above his professional accomplishments. For these reasons, most of all, this book is dedicated in his honor.

Finally, as a personal notation, although this work is intended to help advanced doctoral students and postdoctoral residents in psychology prepare for licensure as psychologists, I acknowledge the many critical shortcomings of professional licensure. Clearly it would be myopic not to recognize the weaknesses inherent in professional licensing—in psychology and elsewhere. This is an issue, though, that does not ease the preparatory process in any way whatsoever. My concern, and the intention of this book, is not to understand or challenge the process of licensure. Rather, the goal is to help maximize the possibility of successfully completing the examination process. After all, for most candidates interested in the practice of psychology, licensure, once accomplished, can open a world of new opportunities.

All this said and done, let us begin the preparatory process.

T.D.C.

1 Preludes to Preparation

Chapter Preview

WHY BE CONCERNED WITH PREPARATION FOR LICENSURE?

PURPOSE

Candidates for licensure should know that the Examination for Professional Practice in Psychology (EPPP) can be rigorous. The exam is a key hurdle for those interested in becoming licensed psychologists.

STRATEGY

A carefully designed study program can:

- clarify, consolidate, and refresh past learning;
- help candidates learn areas that may have been overlooked or treated less intensively during graduate school;
- help candidates learn the necessary details and areas of focus that are specifically tested in the licensing examination.

TAKING THE EPPP

Each year, graduates from doctoral programs in psychology from throughout the United States sit for the Examination for Professional Practice in Psychology (EPPP), sponsored by the Association of State and Provincial Psychology Boards (formerly the American Association of State Psychology Boards).* Many candidates pass the examination on the first attempt. Many do not. Typically, candidates are knowledgeable in certain areas but lack adequate knowledge or preparation in other areas. For many, the examination evokes feelings of frustration and anxiety.

Nonetheless, clinicians who intend to offer psychological services to the public must be licensed or certified by the state in which they intend to practice. Therefore, candidates who are interested in becoming licensed psychologists must somehow successfully pass the Examination For Professional Practice in Psychology.

Designed by leading psychologists from throughout the United States, the EPPP is administered annually in April and October. It is a multiple-choice examination in which candidates select one answer for each question. Comprised of 200 multiple-choice items, the final score is based on the items answered correctly.

Although generally it is considered one of the more significant challenges to licensure, the EPPP was not designed to serve as the sole standard for licensure. Nor is it the exclusive criterion for licensure. Licensing boards review educational backgrounds of candidates, ensure that each candidate possesses coursework in clearly defined areas of psychology, review professional training (such as practicum, fieldwork, internship training, and postdoctorate residency experiences), and often individual states will augment the EPPP with an oral examination, essay examination, or a multiple-choice examination involving

---

*Because psychology, at the independent practice level, is recognized as a doctoral degree profession, this text is addressed largely to candidates with doctorates. It is certainly acknowledged, however, that a few states, including Alaska, Vermont, and Maine, license graduates with master's degrees, and the information as outlined may also be of interest to a number of these candidates. Candidates should use that which is useful and informative and discard that which is not applicable.

state laws and/or issues specifically tailored to practice in that locale. However, because the EPPP is so widely utilized, most candidates associate it with licensure.

Successful completion of the EPPP, then, addresses only one of a series of requisites to becoming a licensed psychologist. However, because of the importance of the EPPP, a large focus of our attention in this book will involve the general areas addressed by the EPPP. At the same time, because there are qualifying standards and requirements, and because individual states often supplement the EPPP with additional examination procedures, these areas are also addressed.

Licensure does rest heavily on successful completion of the EPPP, and success can be enhanced through careful study and preparation. It is also important to reiterate that licensure also demands that other standards be met, and candidates should ensure that they meet all the standards. In fact, as licensing standards become increasingly rigorous, stories about candidates with doctorates who are denied entrance to the national examination because of specific shortcomings in their background will likely continue.

In short, although the EPPP is not the sole criterion for licensure, it is an icon and represents one of the final hurdles to becoming a licensed psychologist.

EXAMINATION PROFICIENCY

Licensure is not important only for psychologists; it is important also for the public as a way to identify competent professionals who have completed appropriate education and training for professional practice. However, highly competent candidates can experience frustration in completing the licensing examination. Needless to say, the reasons that candidates are not successful can involve a host of variables, from examsmanship, to anxiety, to poor test preparation strategies, to an overly exacting command of knowledge in one area of psychology and a weaker command of knowledge in another area.

Fortunately, most candidates actually have a good likelihood of successfully completing the examination. Truly, the examination process is passable! Like most things of value, though, something of such distinction will not come without some measure of personal sacrifice.

Most licensure candidates, whether trained in clinical psychology, school psychology, counseling psychology, or industrial/organizational psychology can expect an examination that, although certainly encompassing, is not necessarily insurmountable. The successful candidate, barring the stellar individuals who can, and often do, dazzle the world with their brilliance, will need to systematically organize a program of preparation and study. It should be emphasized, however, that no matter how prestigious the university or professional school where the candidate was trained, the responsibility for attaining licensure rests totally with each applicant. Candidates often do not fully recognize this fact and mistakenly believe that, having received their professional degrees, they will somehow draw from their accumulated knowledge and pass the EPPP with ease.

Forewarned is Forearmed

The EPPP is a rigorous examination. Those who successfully complete the examination have established licensure and the examination as priorities. You must decide. How important is licensure to you?

EDUCATIONAL REQUIREMENTS FOR LICENSURE

In a society that increasingly places importance on professional licensure and certification, appropriate training and academic preparation can no longer be taken for granted. Too often, graduates—perhaps a newly minted Ph.D. in clinical psychology—discover that they are not eligible for licensure. The news can be devastating.

Although this book's purpose is to provide preparation strategies for eligible candidates, it would be remiss not to provide the reader with an explanation of the general requirements necessary to achieve licensure. This information will be of particular interest to three groups: doctoral degree students completing graduate and postdoctoral training, licensure candidates

Self-Assessment Exercise 1-1

Write three reasons why licensure is important to you. Be specific. Remember that licensure can be important for different reasons. For one person, licensure may involve financial opportunities; for another, it may offer the autonomy of independent practice. State *your* reasons.

_____

_____

_____

Self-Assessment Exercise 1-2

Use this space to identify two reasons that other candidates might fail.

_____

_____

_____

Now, list two reasons that could hamper your performance. Be honest with yourself!

_____

_____

_____

actively preparing for the national examination, and postdoctoral students pursuing doctoral respecialization programs in professional psychology.

GENERAL REVIEW OF REQUIREMENTS FOR LICENSURE

Licensure candidates in psychology should recognize that state statutes, by and large, require a doctoral degree in psychology (Ph.D., Ed.D., Psy.D.) from a university or professional school with regional accreditation.

Although the statutes vary somewhat (a number of states allow candidates with doctoral degrees from programs "substantially psychological in nature" to take the examination), increasingly, the doctoral degree is expected to be from a psychology program in a university or professional school with regional accreditation. The ramifications of this requirement should be understood clearly: A candidate who has a Ph.D. in clinical psychology from a university that has state accreditation but lacks regional accreditation would not be eligible for licensure. Likewise, a candidate with a Ph.D. from a program in counselor education rather than counseling psychology could also be deemed ineligible for licensure.

Unfortunately, many students do not learn such particulars until they have completed graduate work. Too often, this is too late and, if licensure remains a goal, the candidate must subsequently pursue another program that meets the standards.

DOCUMENTED PROGRAM IN PSYCHOLOGY.

Candidates need to recognize that the university program of study must be a documented program in psychology. Program accreditation from the American Psychological Association is one sound indication of such documentation. Questions are often raised, however, as to how documentation is defined. The following listing, organized along lines similar to those typically found in state statutes, provides guidelines that commonly are used by regulatory boards:

1. The program must be identified clearly as a psychology program and identified as such in institutional publications.

Self-Assessment Exercise 1-3

Is your doctoral degree "license eligible"?

_____

_____

Does the university or professional school of psychology in which the program is housed possess *regional* accreditation?

_____

_____

Have you acquired state statutory requirements from the licensing board in the state in which you intend to practice?

_____

_____

2. The program must stand as a coherent organizational entity within the school or university.
3. The program must offer an integrated sequence of study.
4. The program must possess an identifiable faculty of psychologists and be under the authority of a psychologist.
5. The program must have an identifiable body of students matriculated for a degree.
6. The program must include practica, internships, and professional training applicable to the practice of psychology.
7. The program must encompass a minimum of three years of full-time study.

Self-Assessment Exercise 1-4

Is your doctoral degree from a program that is identified clearly as a "psychology" program?

_____

_____

Have past graduates secured licensure as psychologists in the state in which they intend to practice? List any whom you know.

_____

_____

_____

_____

_____

_____

Prior to initiating a comprehensive program of study, students should contact the Board of Examiners of Psychologists in the state in which they plan to practice, and should secure a copy of state regulatory requirements. After studying the statutes, any possible areas of deficit should be investigated. Don't assume eligibility: clarify your education and training.

SUBSTANTIVE CURRICULUM IN PROFESSIONAL PSYCHOLOGY.

Typically, candidates must be able to document educational study in several specific areas. It is expected that three of the four areas on the following list should be addressed. Candidates should be aware, however, that requirements vary from state to state, and for some specialty certifications all four substantive areas are expected to have been addressed. Substantive core areas, with examples of qualifying coursework, are:

- biological bases of behavior, which may include neuropsychology, psychopharmacology, physiological psychology, or comparative psychology;
- cognitive-affective bases of behavior, which may involve coursework in learning, thinking, or motivation, or in emotional social bases of behavior, which can include social psychology, group processes, or organizational and systems theory;
- individual differences, which may involve personality theory, human development, or abnormal psychology.

In addition to these substantive core areas, it is expected that candidates also will have received academic and professional instruction in (1) research design and methodology, (2) statistics and psychometrics, and (3) ethics and professional standards.

PRE- AND POSTDOCTORAL EXPERIENTIAL TRAINING.

In addition to the substantive educational requirements listed above, candidates must document certain experiential training requirements. Traditionally, this involves documentation totaling two years of professional field experience. Generally, this includes one year of predoctoral training (which need not necessarily be completed in one calendar year) as well as one year of postdoctoral supervision (which also need not be completed necessarily during one calendar year but, at minimum, must be accomplished within a period of two consecutive years).

In addition to the general requirement of field experience are several specific areas that can vary from state to state and occasionally present problems to candidates. By and large, it is acceptable to gain predoctoral field experiences through a variety of avenues: practicum, internship, or field training. However, these experiences must be supervised by a professional psychologist and must meet a minimum number of hourly requirements stipulated by statute. This is largely of minimal concern,

Self-Assessment Exercise 1-5

Identify specific courses you have completed that meet the criteria for each area of study required for licensure.

_____

_____

_____

_____

_____

_____

Compare your training against state regulatory requirements, and list areas that require further coursework.

_____

_____

_____

_____

however, for individuals who complete internship programs approved by the American Psychological Association, as these training programs regulate the quality of training and supervision.

Not all students understand the possible internship approaches, though. A student could, for instance, earn a Ph.D. in clinical psychology from a university without accreditation from the American Psychological Association (APA) but complete an internship with accreditation from APA. Similarly, a student might earn an Ed.D. in counseling psychology from a university with APA accreditation but complete an internship without APA accreditation. Fortunately, in these examples, both candidates could be approved for licensure.

If any potential concerns arise, it is best to check individual state statutes or to contact individual state licensing boards. Moreover, for the areas of clinical psychology, school psychology, and counseling psychology, internship training should total a minimum of 1,500 hours of supervised experience.

Postdoctoral training must be supervised by a licensed professional psychologist, supervision must involve weekly

Self-Assessment Exercise 1-6

Did your internship meet the requirements for licensure?

_____

Did you acquire the required number of hours of professional service?

_____

Did you receive adequate face-to-face supervision?

_____

Do you foresee any problems?

_____

face-to-face contact, and the experience must involve work experience appropriate to professional practice.

If candidates are graduates of a university or professional school program approved by the American Psychological Association, and if the internship is completed in a program accredited by APA, candidates are usually in sound shape. However, graduates of APA programs sometimes can encounter difficulty if the postdoctoral internship or residency training falls below the mark.

PRIORITIZING FOR SUCCESS

Most people juggle a variety of priorities on a daily basis. Usually candidates know this. As graduate students and interns, most candidates were faced with a variety of differing responsibilities and commitments. It is not uncommon, for example, for graduate students to balance a full academic courseload, part-time clinical responsibilities, and sometimes a part-time job. Some students think such a heavy work load will end after they receive their degree. In many ways, though, life can become more demanding after graduation.

Often, with the receipt of a doctoral degree, comes a geographic relocation, a job, and a redefinition of personal relationships. At the same time, preparing for licensure demands time and energy for rigorous study. Such demands, quite naturally, can exact a toll. Some candidates react by resisting, avoiding, and procrastinating. However, there are strategies that can help to counteract such inclinations.

Key Point to Remember: Design a preparatory plan.

Preparatory Planning: Building a Foundation for Success

Design a study plan using the following worksheet. Decide how much time each day and each week you can devote to study for licensure. Be specific and realistic. Consider the variables in your life.

Key Point to Remember: Designing a workable and realistic study plan is a challenging enterprise. It is a good idea to plan a mock test for your study plan. Note your weaknesses and adapt and refine as necessary. Build a study program that can work for you.

Establish Study Periods.

Because you will be studying a vast amount of information, it is wise to establish standardized times when you can study. You

Weekly Time Management Worksheet

Name: _____

Date of Licensure Exam: _____

Weekly Study Topic: _____

Total Planned Study Time: _____

Time	Task						
	Sun	Mon	Tues	Wed	Thur	Fri	Sat
5:00 A.M.							
6:00							
7:00							
8:00							
9:00							
10:00							
11:00							
Noon							
1:00 P.M.							
2:00							
3:00							
4:00							
5:00							
6:00							
7:00							
8:00							
9:00							
10:00							

may choose to study for 60 minutes before work and 60 minutes after work—even before you leave your office. Or you may choose to study in the evenings.

Distributed periods of study will accomplish far more than large massed blocks of study time. For example, musicians may practice one, two, or three hours daily, but very few successful musicians would try to practice one day a week, no matter how long they might plan to study and practice on that occasion. Distributed study is simply more effective, although it can be enhanced when used in conjunction with periodic periods of massed study.

Despite this knowledge, coordinating multiple life tasks can be challenging. Other variables, such as family responsibilities or vocational interests, also can create obstacles to study. As you select and plan your study times, consider competing life alternatives and outline your needs realistically.

Key Point to Remember: For success, consider the concept of "special" study periods where study time has priority over all other tasks. Make these times a priority. Despite any temptations or inclinations to avoid study, establish "safe" study time blocks.

SET LARGE WEEKLY STUDY BLOCKS.

Because you must review and often learn complex blocks of information from several areas of psychology, it is helpful to augment daily study blocks with time periods when you have the opportunity to study uninterrupted for longer periods of time. Because of the highly complex nature of specific exam questions, longer study blocks can also be used for mock examinations. These should be scheduled and planned and will require a minimum of four consecutive, uninterrupted hours of time. This does not even include time to score and review results.

Key Point to Remember: Look for two time periods each week when you can study without interruption for long periods of time. Use these times to completely immerse yourself in study. Choose times when you will feel relaxed.

PLAN REST PERIODS.

Understand that study is taxing, physically and emotionally. Rest is important; don't run on empty. In fact, it can be helpful

Self-Assessment Exercise 1-7

Consider how you will feel about studying in such an intense, structured way over the months ahead. Write down your feelings.

_____

_____

_____

Self-Assessment Exercise 1-8

It is important to recognize the important role that recreation and leisure occupy in psychological well-being. Often, we think coursework and study should somehow be times of unending scholarly (monastic) endeavor. This is nonsense. Work and play can mutually coexist. What are two activities you find relaxing?

_____

_____

to plan recreational activities on a regular basis. Consider incorporating these activities into your study plan. Ideally these will follow study time blocks, serving as a reward and reinforcing your efforts. Typically, it is more difficult to study after a day at the beach or skiing in the mountains than it is to study before enjoying a leisure break. You can avoid frustration by studying first and playing later.

Key Point to Remember: Do not take your need for rest and recreation lightly. Plan time periods when you can freely participate in activities that will bring pleasure to your life. Your ability to relax and enjoy life can truly help maintain a healthy and positive attitude during this examination preparation period. Plan both study periods and rest periods.

APPLY AN ORGANIZED STUDY PROGRAM.

As most psychologists who recently have passed the Examination for Professional Practice in Psychology can attest, licensure tests a far-reaching scope of knowledge. Don't approach study for the EPPP in a hit-or-miss fashion; choose your study material carefully. Many candidates can prepare by using individually designed study materials. That's a good way, but there are also well-designed commercially available study programs that can be used as a basis for systematic preparation and can be purchased separately or in conjunction with classroom study. Choose your materials as carefully as you would for a graduate program. The intensity of your effort can be enhanced or diminished by the quality of materials you use.

Key Point to Remember: Your preparation program can only be effective with well-designed, focused, relevant study ma-

Self-Assessment Exercise 1-9

Needless to say, each candidate for licensure will have unique needs. Would a self-designed review program or a commercially marketed program be most effective for you? List your preferences.

_____

_____

_____

terials. Consider selecting or designing materials that can most effectively be of use to you. To do anything else will only compromise your commitment. Your effort is only as good as your material.

COMMIT YOURSELF TO LICENSURE.

In some professions, many licensure candidates give only a token commitment to licensure or certification. In part, this is why many accountants do not pass the certified public accountant (CPA) examination on their first attempt. It may also explain why a number of law school graduates repeatedly experience frustration with the bar examination. The point is that

---

Self-Assessment Exercise 1-10

List the variables that enhance your sense of commitment to successfully completing the licensure examination. How committed are you?

_____

_____

What personal sense of satisfaction can licensure bring?

_____

_____

What effect might licensure have on your life?

_____

_____

successful candidates, by and large, set licensure as a priority and demonstrate the necessary commitment to their goals. Although certainly there are other activities more pleasurable than preparing for licensure, successful candidates must make certain sacrifices to achieve their objective.

Key Point to Remember: Commitment is an undisputed key to successfully passing the Examination for Professional Practice in Psychology. Think back to the years of study and work you

---

Self-Assessment Exercise 1-11

Examine your support network. Is there a study or support group in your area?

_____

Would your state psychological association be a useful contact for forming (or locating) a study and support group?

_____

Self-Assessment Exercise 1-12

Consider these questions carefully: Have you explained to your family and friends the important role which their support can make in helping you reach the licensure goal?

_____

Do you think that attending a review course might offer certain opportunities to meet others undergoing preparation?

_____

committed while pursuing your doctorate. Licensure is the final hurdle. Maintain your commitment and savor the final reward.

DEVELOP A SUPPORT NETWORK.

Unfortunately, for many candidates, licensure often is attempted alone. Usually this occurs because candidates are no longer part of a university or professional school community or no longer have the same network of colleagues and friends. Nevertheless, it is vital to establish a supportive professional team.

Key Point to Remember: Both personal and professional support networks can be enormously helpful for licensure candidates. No woman or man is an island; usually multiple supportive contacts can be developed. Recognize the positive benefits of a support team and develop a team to help you reach your goal.

CONDUCT MOCK EXAMINATIONS.

You should plan practice (mock) test examinations periodically. Ideally, these practice exams should be taken away from home, possibly in a university library, a local public library, or in some sort of a classroom setting with an atmosphere similar to that you will experience when you actually sit for the licensure examination in your state. Chart your progress, assess your strengths, and evaluate your weaknesses.

Key Point to Remember: Mock examinations can be enormously useful to licensure candidates by helping to simulate the examination process, by providing opportunities to become assimilated to the physical and psychological rigors of the licensing examination, and by offering opportunities to highlight and evaluate strengths and weaknesses. Candidates should make mock examinations as realistic as possible.

USE NOTECARDS FOR KEY POINTS.

Typically, most licensure candidates confront areas of knowledge that will require continuing review—overlearning. These points can be written on notecards that can be kept in a pocket. These helpful cards can be utilized in a variety of different situations to enhance learning and memory storage.

Developing a notecard system to enhance study efforts involves a minimal degree of effort. Nobody's memory is so well de-

Self-Assessment Exercise 1-13

The practice of mock examinations is an important learning tool. Where might you take a mock examination?

_____

How can mock examinations help you?

_____

_____

Briefly outline your strengths as a licensure candidate: How will you respond as you identify areas of weakness?

_____

_____

veloped that such a simple system would not benefit it. You can use notecards to learn differing statistical designs, to clearly learn critical facts, and to provide organizational structure to your thinking.

Key Point to Remember: A notecard system designed for individual needs can offer an unprecedented opportunity to learn and overlearn. Notecards can be used easily in a vast array of situations to help maximize learning.

USE TIME EFFICIENTLY.

Becoming a licensed psychologist requires diligence, study, and time management. Learning to study and use time efficiently can maximize learning, reduce frustration, and help provide a unifying fabric to preparation. At best, you can organize your life so that stress is minimized. Without efficient (and effective)

Self-Assessment Exercise 1-14

How efficient are you?

_____

Are you well-organized?

_____

Do you wait to the last minute to complete tasks?

_____

time management, licensure preparation can become needlessly frustrating. Use an organized preparatory map to reach your goals. Write your honest answers to the following questions.

Key Point to Remember: An efficient preparatory study program can be designed with the help of effective time management. Clearly, time management can reduce stress, provide structure, and maximize human resources.

CONCLUSIONS

Think back to the key points emphasized in this chapter. How motivated are you to achieving licensure? Have you considered designing a daily, as well as a weekly, study schedule?

Unfortunately, although most psychologists can cognitively appreciate the value of time management and weekly study schedules, many do not use such designs to help achieve

Self-Assessment Exercise 1-15

Would you benefit from enhanced planning?

_____

Did you approach your dissertation in an organized, time-efficient manner?

_____

Identify two occasions when you were disorganized and used your time inefficiently.

_____

_____

What were two occasions when you were well-organized and used your time efficiently?

_____

_____

List two or three reasons that you were so well-organized.

_____

_____

_____

What or who specifically helped you?

_____

_____

_____

_____

their own goals. A well-designed study plan, though, can be used to achieve our goals with surprising ease.

Our task is to design a plan which can maximize learning and, at the same time, can maximize the probabilities of successfully attaining licensure as a psychologist. Toward this end, 10 strategies were identified in this chapter:

1. Design a study plan.
2. Establish study periods.
3. Set large weekly study blocks.
4. Plan rest periods.
5. Apply an organized study program.
6. Commit yourself to licensure.
7. Develop a support network.
8. Conduct mock examinations.
9. Use a notecard system for key points.
10. Use time efficiently.

Licensure, unequivocally, is a challenge for virtually every psychologist. As you start planning your study schedule, use your knowledge of and skill in educational psychology to maximize your learning. More to the point, design a realistic schedule that fits your situation. Although some candidates may find it best to study in their offices an hour before work and an hour after work, others may find it most helpful to exercise early each morning and to study two hours between 7:00 and 9:00 each evening. What is best and most appropriate for you? Can you maintain your study schedule? Can you schedule sufficient time, daily and weekly, to achieve your objectives? Do you have a support network? These questions are important and the answers are critical.

At this point, it is a good idea to review your Weekly Time Management Worksheet. There are probably areas that need change. Use the following time management worksheet to revise your initial schedule. Develop a realistic guide that you can use every day.

Weekly Time Management Worksheet

Name: _____

Date of Licensure Examination: _____

Area of Study: _____

Considerations:

___ (1) study plan   ___ (6) commitment

___ (2) study periods   ___ (7) support network

___ (3) longer weekly study blocks   ___ (8) mock examinations

___ (4) rest periods   ___ (9) notecard system

___ (5) organized study program   ___ (10) time efficiency

				Task			
Time	Sun	Mon	Tues	Wed	Thur	Fri	Sat
5:00 A.M.							
6:00							
7:00							
8:00							
9:00							
10:00							
11:00							
Noon							
1:00 P.M.							
2:00							
3:00							
4:00							
5:00							
6:00							
7:00							
8:00							
9:00							
10:00							

2 Goalsetting for Licensure

Chapter Preview

How goalsetting can help you prepare for licensure

Purpose

Candidates for licensure should know that goalsetting can serve as a roadmap to success, highlighting small achievements and reinforcing efforts toward long-term goals.

Strategy

Goalsetting can:

- improve performance;
- focus study efforts;
- enhance confidence;
- identify targets for success.

GOAL-SETTING STRATEGIES

Preparatory study may be designed by the learner, or it can be designed by others. This is especially true for licensure candidates who can select traditional seminar/classroom preparatory programs, choose sequenced self-study programs, or design individualized study programs. Whatever approach is chosen, though, candidates are ultimately responsible for their individual attainment of knowledge.

You are responsible for determining the importance of licensure in your future. You are responsible for selecting or designing a plan that will help you to attain your goal. You are responsible for designing your own roadmap. Goal-setting strategies can help.

This chapter is aimed at expanding your knowledge of goalsetting. It is designed to link goalsetting with preparatory efforts for candidates for licensure in psychology.

Constructing goals in a clear, consistent, and logical fashion and negotiating a framework that can enhance the available opportunities for achieving goals are keys to learning and development. However, although it is a useful concept, most people actually know very little about goalsetting.

The goal of this chapter, therefore, is to help candidates better understand key considerations which underlie goalsetting. So often, more times than most of us care to admit, people do not reach their goals, not necessarily because their goal is unattainable, but because the foundation upon which the goal was constructed was shaky. Many people do not even realize this, so they waste time, energy, and effort.

More than likely, goalsetting was involved in the successful achievement of your doctoral program. To demonstrate the tremendous focusing power of goalsetting, the following example may be illuminating.

I have been especially impressed by the goal-setting techniques of world-class skiers and mountain climbers. Not only do world-class skiers set lofty goals, they often achieve even higher goals than they initially set. We can see this when we observe world-class skiers in action. Sometimes, you almost pity the mountain!

On close examination, ski champions typically can provide detailed, systematic (sometimes written) roadmaps that were conscientiously developed to reach their goals. In other words, they don't leave success to chance. This is obvious when we observe

Self-Assessment Exercise 2-1

Think about your career and what you hope to accomplish. You probably have a number of goals. Identify three goals for your career.

_____

_____

_____

Is licensure one of your goals?

_____

Where would you rank licensure?

_____

Self-Assessment Exercise 2-2

Think about the steps you took to select a graduate program. List the ingredients that led to your successful completion of your doctoral degree program.

_____

_____

_____

_____

_____

_____

Olympic slalom and freestyle skiers. The former typically commit the race course to memory before slashing out of the starting gate. World champion aerial freestyle skiers, likewise, use visual imagery strategies to maximize their performance. World-class freestyle skiers actually see themselves (in their mind's eye) performing each maneuver *before* they leave the take-off ramp. And they see their goals, as well, as they train and prepare for competition. In short, gold medal performers approach their goals, whether involving a local championship race, a regional competition, or a national title, in a systematic and organized fashion. Winners set goals and winners set about achieving their goals.

Let's look at the mountain climbing community. Climbers negotiating new routes often spend considerable time acclimating to high altitude before pursuing the summit. They also plan their routes. Carefully. World-class climbers train, stock provisions, and carefully plan their assault on the mountain. Champions leave little to chance.

It is true that academic and athletic goals are different, but the process of goalsetting offers a framework we can all use. Goalsetting requires specific skills and a systematic, logical sequence of events. Using the skier illustration, a budding intermediate skier who attempts a world-class downhill course while still perfecting a parallel turn is risking a great deal—physically and emotionally. On the other hand, if the skier's goal is to learn to race, downhill or otherwise, he or she can be systematically coached and taught proper skills to ultimately (assuming adequate physical and psychological conditions are met) negotiate the racecourse at some level of proficiency. World-class skiers routinely use goalsetting.

Most psychologists, at least on an intuitive level, have learned much in the way of goal attainment. The purpose now is to build on that experience and to crystallize the ingredients so that you may more effectively harness the skills needed for licensure. Ten basic tenets or considerations for effective goalsetting are:

1. Goals should be specific.
2. Goals should be measurable.
3. Goals should be compatible.
4. Goals should have clear time frames.
5. Goals should be prioritized.
6. Goals should be verbalized.
7. Goals should be written and stored prominently.

Self-Assessment Exercise 2-3

Licensure candidates can refine their goal-setting skills by focusing on the attainments they already have accomplished. Summarize five major accomplishments you have achieved.

_____

_____

_____

_____

_____

8. Goals should build on past accomplishments.
9. Goals should be flexible.
10. Goals should be evaluated on performance and effort.

Candidates should consider how each individual point on the above list can be of use in preparing for the licensure exam. Look at your major accomplishments. Were any of them goals you had set about achieving? Was goalsetting a part of your efforts? Could goalsetting help you now?

ADAPTING GOALSETTING TO LICENSURE

The practice of setting and achieving personal and professional goals is a key attribute of prosperity, fortune, and achievement. The worst thing professionals can do with their careers is to drift along without a roadmap for success. The winners—those individuals who garner promotions, earn advanced degrees, complete professional certifications, achieve professional satisfac-

Self-Assessment Exercise 2-4

Identify four tenets of goalsetting that you feel are important to your study program and are applicable to you.

_____

_____

_____

_____

Self-Assessment Exercise 2-5

Turn each goal-setting tenet into a question and ask yourself how it fits your life. What will you need to change in your life to achieve licensure?

_____

_____

What will you need to prioritize to achieve licensure?

_____

_____

Can you be flexible and allow licensure to take one or more years of preparation, or should other areas of your life be relegated less importance?

_____

_____

tion, or otherwise experience success—seem particularly skillful at setting and achieving goals.

Virtually all psychologists would like to enjoy personal development. The desire to develop is a phenomenon that pervades the world. Whether you are completing internship training in clinical psychology, finishing course distribution requirements in counseling psychology, or preparing for comprehensive examinations in school psychology, the concept of goal-oriented growth is critical to your individual success.

There really is no magical formula for achieving success, but the course is often paved by small markers of progress (that is, goals). Much like a skier negotiating gates in a slalom course, the markers of progress can serve as benchmarks, leading each person forward and providing assurance that one's ultimate objective is truly obtainable. To adapt goalsetting to fit your study program, consider the following points:

- Specific goals can improve performance.
- Higher performances are elicited from more demanding goals, providing the goals are accepted and desirable.
- Satisfaction correlates with performance. When goals are reached, satisfaction and confidence flourish.

Typically, as goals are accomplished they are modified and refined. Refining is part of the dynamic nature of goalsetting. Specific and measurable goals can instill confidence, guide learning, and motivate development. Those who do this in their work find their progress defined by sequential attainments. Although not everyone will embrace each concept for goalsetting, a richer appreciation for success can be gained when you pay attention to the relationships between performance, success, and goalsetting.

A developmental framework is suggested below for candidates who are interested in incorporating goal-setting strategies into their licensure study programs. In considering the design framework, you should review the way each ingredient may have been involved in your past learning.

Framework for Setting Goals

Successful athletes know that when goals are too high or unrealistic they are less likely to experience success. Failure decreases performance and diminishes self-esteem. Likewise, success is contagious, enhancing self-esteem and providing a foundation for further development.

Candidates for psychology licensure will find it useful to consider both long-term and short-term goals. The framework that follows offers one perspective for developing a plan using a combination of both short- and long-term goals as challenges.

DEVELOP MICROGOALS.

Everyone enjoys experiencing success. It feels good and helps improve motivation. Microgoals are designed to be achieved in roughly an hour or less. Such goals are immediately reinforcing, and they instill confidence.

It is helpful to continually set small achievable goals. Decide how you might incorporate them into your study program. It may be useful, for example, to mentally break practice exami-

---

Self-Assessment Exercise 2-6

Consider how you might break your study efforts into short functional units. Identify two areas you could study in this fashion.

_____

_____

Identify two ways you might feel strengthened after studying short units of knowledge.

_____

_____

nations into several miniexaminations. Or you may find it useful to study pieces and segments that were tested by the examination, part by part. As an example, you might study parametric statistics one day, and nonparametric statistics the next day, rather than everything all at once. You might even allow a 5- or 10-minute break between each section.

It is important to realize that preparation for the licensure examination accommodates the micro-goal-setting procedure. Professional ethics, for instance, an area that comprises approximately 16.5% of the examination, can be organized into several sections by studying one, two, or three ethical guidelines in each study session.

ESTABLISH MINIGOALS.

Some tasks simply cannot be mastered in an hour. Minigoals may take from one day to a month to achieve. Completing a

Self-Assessment Exercise 2-7

How could you use microgoals to study professional ethics?

_____

_____

Would it be helpful to study each ethical guideline in this fashion?

_____

_____

Would it be helpful to use notecards?

_____

thorough review of industrial psychology, learning about performance appraisal methodology, and understanding the strengths and limitations of work samples are examples of minigoals that typically cannot be accomplished in less than a day.

Minigoals, then, are indispensable in understanding goalsetting, because some tasks require more time for completion. A licensure preparation program simply cannot be completed in one day. Fortunately, minigoals can serve as an important bridge, and they may be composed of several microgoals that are designed to enhance success.

PLAN SHORT-RANGE GOALS.

Goals that take one month to a year to complete are, for our purposes, identified as short-range goals. Examples of short-range goals might include the completion of a doctoral dissertation or

Self-Assessment Exercise 2-8

Summarize your feelings about accepting the reality that licensure examines concepts and principles that cannot be learned or reviewed in a day. What key areas do you already know that will require this kind of attention?

_____

_____

_____

_____

_____

the development and implementation of a program evaluation system on a psychiatric unit. Each accomplishment requires time. Success-oriented people recognize that time is a valuable part of growth and development. Just as a child cannot be rushed through certain developmental phases such as learning to walk, so, too, short-range goals cannot be circumvented.

In today's fast-paced world, many people lack patience. Unfortunately, one must accept reality; certain goals cannot be rushed. Psychologists interested in licensure know this, because licensure candidates must complete graduate training that simply cannot be completed in a fortnight.

ANALYZE MEDIUM-RANGE GOALS.

Goals that span a time period of up to five years are classified as medium-range goals. Typically, medium-range goals encompass long-term education or training. Individuals who have secured 3, 4, and possibly 5-year car financing loans can grasp the concept immediately. Medium-range goals can take years to accomplish. Doctoral programs are illustrative of medium-range goals.

Self-Assessment Exercise 2-9

How many months do you feel you realistically will need to effectively prepare for licensure?

_____

Are there any areas which will require more than a month to master?

_____

_____

_____

Although often frustrating for people looking for immediate rewards, medium-range goals serve as important markers of accomplishment and should be duly acknowledged on completion. Postdoctoral training in psychoanalytic treatment or forensic psychology are examples of goals that can take several years to accomplish.

Curiously, despite the fact that psychologists recognize that doctoral training is itself a medium-range goal, licensure candidates do not always recognize the long-term nature of licensure.

CONSIDER LONG-RANGE GOALS.

Goals that pertain to a life style or an overall life map are classified as long-range goals. It is important to remain flexible with

---

Self-Assessment Exercise 2-10

How many years are required to acquire licensure? Include predoctoral and postdoctoral field experiences.

_____

How would you feel if it would take two years of study to successfully pass the licensure examination? Would you give up, as some clients do in frustration when told that a particular interpersonal problem may take more than one or two sessions to resolve? Or would you rally to the challenge? What are your feelings about medium-range goals?

_____

_____

_____

long-range goals and consider what long-term objectives are desired over a lifetime. This practice helps provide a foundation for future growth and development.

Long-range goals can vary dramatically. The ideal lifestyle for a neuropsychologist in a large metropolitan hospital in San Francisco would certainly differ from a school psychologist practicing in an elementary school in Park City, Utah, or from a clinical psychologist developing a private practice in Brattleboro, Vermont.

Because of the wide differences in life-oriented goals, it is important that people recognize certain basic values and orientations. A business consultant who has completed a master of business administration degree at Stanford University and who subsequently pursues a doctorate in industrial-organizational psychology at the California School of Professional Psychology may possess a markedly different life map than a graduate student in clinical psychology at the University of Vermont who is preparing to practice in a rural mental health clinic. From their work hours to their benefits, the overall career life-style of these individuals, although both are psychologists, may differ considerably.

Long-range goals for licensed psychologists can certainly demonstrate considerable diversity, and this is exactly why so many choose psychology as a career. Simply put, the diversity is compelling. In fact, many psychologists combine different work settings, combining part-time work in a community mental health clinic, for instance, with a small private practice.

At the same time, whether trained in a university or professional school, or pursuing specialty work in such areas as health psychology, neuropsychology, family psychology, and community psychology, most psychologists with interests involving direct services recognize the necessity of licensure.

CONCLUSIONS

Too few people in all endeavors map out clear and written goals for their lives. One way of reaching one's dreams, though, is through goalsetting. Indeed, when goals are achieved, confidence and self-esteem rises. For athletes and sports participants, this

Self-Assessment Exercise 2-11

List three ways that licensure may enhance your career over the next 25 years.

_____

_____

_____

What do you think would be the long-term implications of not achieving licensure?

_____

_____

has the benefit of enhancing performance. For candidates for licensure in psychology, goalsetting can serve as a roadmap to success.

Although goalsetting is not particularly complex, the task is surprising in its long-range implications. For thousands of professionals from all walks of life, goalsetting can provide a bridge for long-range dreams. In this chapter, goalsetting was explored as a useful framework organizing study strategies. Specifically, ten basic considerations were highlighted:

1. Write specific goals.
2. Use goals that can be measured.
3. Choose compatible goals.
4. Select goals that have clear time frames.
5. Determine priorities for goals.
6. Be able to verbalize goals.
7. Write and store goals prominently.
8. Build on past accomplishments.

Self-Assessment Exercise 2-12

What would be the effect of delaying, rather than failing, licensure?

_____

_____

How important is licensure to your immediate future?

_____

_____

How important is licensure to your long-term goals?

_____

_____

How much commitment do you need to make to achieve these goals?

_____

_____

9. Keep goals flexible.
10. Evaluate goals on performance and effort.

It is too early to tell whether we shall each achieve the goals we set for this day, month, year, and beyond. We can hope, of course, that we will all set specific, achievable goals that will bring positive and rewarding feelings of success. Some people, however, invariably will choose to drift through life, lamenting their jobs, frustrating their employers, and generally trusting luck and good fortune for any successes that pass their way.

Drifting aimlessly does not specifically breed success. Builders and architects use detailed plans for major construction efforts. So, too, world-class athletes use carefully designed training plans that address a vast array of factors, ranging from diet to sleeping patterns.

For virtually everyone in society, goalsetting can provide a foundation for development. Designed thoughtfully, with attention to both day-to-day and long-term needs, goalsetting can serve as a map for success. When goals are specific, achievable, and measurable, the process is enlightening. Plan your goals and work your plan.

Self-Assessment Exercise 2-13

Do you have a preparatory program for licensure, right now, that would make your goal a reality? What is it?

_____

_____

_____

Are you planning a gold medal performance on the licensure examination?

_____

_____

3 Assessing Personal Strengths

Chapter Preview

HOW CAN YOUR STRENGTHS HELP YOU TO PREPARE FOR LICENSURE?

PURPOSE

Candidates for licensure should know that it is strategically wise to capitalize on personal strengths, rather than personal weaknesses, to optimize test performance.

STRATEGY

Personal strengths can serve to:

- identify proven study strategies;
- provide a foundation for new learning;
- highlight realistic learning approaches;
- illuminate keys to a winning performance.

IDENTIFYING PERSONAL STRENGTHS

If you are considering developing a systematic study program for licensure, you surely are interested in maximizing your chances for a successful performance. To help prepare for a positive performance, start by assessing your personal strengths. Knowing your strengths means understanding your weaknesses.

Don't use study strategies that are not effective for you. Use what has proven successful. Too many people waste time and energy by relearning what they already know and using ineffective strategies. You should identify study strategies that you have found effective.

Some students study effectively at certain times and places but ineffectively at other times and places. It is important to learn to identify times and places that are effective for you.

Start by looking at study times. There is great individual variation in the times of day and week that different individuals find best to study. Some study best before going to work, others after work. You may study best for an hour before work and an hour after work, or perhaps late at night. Maybe you study best when you have a big bowl of popcorn or dish of ice cream at your side.

Self-Assessment Exercise 3-1

Examine your past study habits and identify the times you studied most effectively. What time was best for you to study: mornings, afternoons, or weekends?

_____

_____

What times were you unable to study successfully?

_____

_____

Self-Assessment Exercise 3-2

Identify the ingredients important to your success. What courses did you excel in at college?

_____

_____

_____

_____

What was positive about those courses?

_____

_____

_____

_____

What motivated you?

_____

_____

_____

_____

Did you do best in the morning, afternoon, or evening?

_____

_____

Self-Assessment Exercise 3-3

List any scholarships or honors you have won.

_____

_____

_____

_____

_____

Identify the reasons you won these honors. Include those qualities you think helped you earn them.

_____

_____

_____

_____

_____

Don't force yourself to study like someone else. Write down the times you have been able to study successfully and match these proven times to your current schedule.

Time isn't everything, though. There are other ingredients you will need to be successful. Be honest. Truthfully, do you feel apprehensive about studying for the licensure examination? If not, you are lucky. If you do, you are not alone. Many people feel apprehensive about studying. That is why so many students procrastinate and put off study. Others study but cannot eliminate

Self-Assessment Exercise 3-4

What extracurricular activities have you enjoyed?

_____

_____

_____

_____

What do you enjoy about these activities?

_____

_____

_____

Why do you continue to participate?

_____

_____

_____

How do you adapt your work schedule and other responsibilities
to accommodate your interests?

_____

_____

_____

Self-Assessment Exercise 3-5

What it is that motivates and makes you persevere?

_____

_____

_____

_____

_____

Were there any commonalities to your successes?

_____

_____

_____

_____

_____

Was the time of day that you participated important? If so, identify that ingredient. If not, identify the ingredient that was important.

_____

_____

_____

_____

Self-Assessment Exercise 3-6

What will make you feel good about your study efforts?

_____

_____

_____

_____

What will help as you prepare for licensure as a psychologist?

_____

_____

_____

Self-Assessment Exercise 3-7

Reread the questions in self-assessment exercises 1 through 6. Look at the times you succeeded and the places and circumstances. List the key ingredients to your successes.

_____

_____

_____

_____

_____

feelings of tenseness and anxiety. A realistic, effective study program that uses your strengths can help relieve the apprehension.

Let's proceed by exploring the specific times that you were effective as a student, identifying specific strengths you can use to prepare for the licensing examination.

STRUCTURING YOUR STRENGTHS

The questions in the self-assessment exercises above are designed to help candidates for licensure conduct their personal inventories and to identify the qualities, attributes, and values that helped in achieving goals and advancing professional careers.

Self-Development Study Form

The following study form will help you to integrate the times, places, circumstances, and key ingredients into a useful motivational strategy.

On the Motivational Study Card below, list answers to the following questions: (1) *reasons* that licensure is important; (2) personal *strengths* you have demonstrated when pursuing a challenging task; (3) *times* when you wanted to give up or stop something, but didn't; (4) something about the *desire* for licensure that you feel good about; and (5) the *examination date.*

Motivational Study Card

REASONS: _____

STRENGTHS: _____

TIMES: _____

DESIRE: _____

EXAM DATE: _____

Using the Motivational Study Card you developed above, copy a set of five identical cards. Put one motivational study card in your wallet or pocketbook; clip a second card to your study materials; put a third card on your refrigerator door (that's right); put a fourth card near your desk; and put the fifth card in a place where you're sure to see it every day (you might put it in your car or on a bathroom mirror).

ESTABLISHING RITUALS

There is no doubt that steady, structured study can pay off. Better yet, students who establish and maintain regular periods of uninterrupted study can amass considerable information. Slow and steady does win the race.

Except for a few gifted individuals, most psychologists pursuing licensure will find it beneficial to establish predictable patterns of study. That is one reason that a study schedule is so important. It is also the reason that certain musicians, artists, and authors are successful. Successful musicians don't practice their craft in a hit or miss fashion. They practice every day, day in and day out. Artists do the same. Successful artists practice their craft daily until it becomes something of a ritual.

When I began working on this book, I jogged each morning. It became a ritual. My jogging and my writing became a part of my life, and my life was oriented around these activities.

Attempting to develop an effective study program can be challenging, and it helps to tap your strengths. In this section, attention has been given to certain proven strategies that you have already found effective. They are still challenging, because most people—even psychologists—are not always exactly certain how they best study and learn. That's why we have suggested different self-assessment questions.

How do people continue with a task even when they don't like something? Fortunately, we have many examples to draw on, including the knowledge that many people work in corporations without finding their work rewarding. But they report to work every day, day after day. Their support systems help. (Okay, pay helps, too.)

Self-Assessment Exercise 3-8

What can you do regularly that you can associate with study, such as jogging, drinking a cup of coffee, and so forth? What will serve as a trigger to study? What will help establish studying as a pattern? What can help you make it a ritual?

_____

_____

_____

_____

Self-Assessment Exercise 3-9

Who can serve as a support system for you and help hold you accountable, daily or weekly, for your studies? List one or two people.

_____

_____

What can you use as an incentive to reward your efforts?

_____

_____

List one or two rewards you would like for your efforts.

_____

_____

_____

CONCLUSIONS

Most candidates for licensure as psychologists possess a number of strengths. Most candidates are extremely intelligent. They have taken many different examinations during their graduate studies, and most come from good, if not excellent, degree programs.

The Examination for Professional Practice in Psychology can be rigorous. Because candidates for the exam come from different programs that are in different places with different orientations, no two candidates bring the same strengths or weaknesses or background experiences to the examination. For example, there are candidates from psychology programs in research universities, from programs at free-standing schools of professional psychology, and from programs housed in schools of education. Some candidates come from small programs that graduate one or two students a year, whereas others come from programs that graduate large numbers of candidates. Each candidate brings individual strengths and weaknesses.

Careful thought should be given, before taking the licensure examination, to designing an effective study program. It is also not too late to design an effective program if you are one of the many who are not successful on the examination on the first attempt.

In assessing your personal strengths that will help you to prepare for licensure, you should:

1. Identify your strengths.
2. Note times and places for effective study.
3. Establish a realistic, effective study program.
4. Structure your strengths.
5. Identify reasons that licensure is important.
6. Establish rituals.
7. Make study a daily part of your life.
8. Identify a personal support system.
9. List reward systems.
10. Maximize the repetition compulsion.

To summarize, candidates should conduct a personal inventory. Carefully identify your strengths. Write down examples that illustrate times you successfully negotiated difficult challenges. Be alert to your hidden strengths. Look for the underlying fabric behind your successes. Look for the rituals. Identify a support network. Maximize the repetition compulsion. And study, study, study.

4 Strategies for Effective Study

Chapter Preview

WHAT STUDY STRATEGIES CAN YOU USE TO MAXIMIZE STUDY?

PURPOSE

Effective study and learning can be exciting. Your task is to identify and study those major areas tested for licensure as a psychologist. Carefully designed study strategies can help you realize your full potential.

STRATEGY

Specific study strategies for licensure can:

- maximize the specificity of effort;
- optimize time and preparatory effort;
- monitor understanding;
- emphasize overlearning;
- assist organizational needs;
- boost concentration;
- reinforce consistent study and learning;
- provide consistency and review.

STUDY STRATEGIES FOR LICENSURE

Study skills are of key importance to candidates for the Examination for Professional Practice in Psychology (EPPP). Certainly, most candidates already possess a certain sophistication in the matter of academic study, and this sensibility is amply demonstrated by the obtainment of a doctoral degree.

An advanced degree, however, is insufficient to secure licensure. Candidates also need to connect and assimilate seemingly disparate areas of psychological knowledge. Melding developmental psychology, clinical psychology, counseling psychology, school psychology, industrial psychology, and social psychology, as well as areas such as professional ethics, can be most challenging. Often, too, the misleading nature of many alternative answers on the examination can be troublesome. Therefore, this chapter will review concrete study tools that can be helpful to candidates preparing for the licensure exam.

Study Pertinent Pieces of Information

Licensure candidates must demonstrate a strong knowledge base. With this in mind, it is particularly important to study examination subject areas you do not know, rather than what you already do know. This is a key point.

Even those candidates with a Ph.D. are fallible in this matter. The focus, the goal, is to pass the examination. Therefore, it is important that you avoid spending time studying areas that you already know exceedingly well while giving little time and effort to areas in which your knowledge may be less than exemplary.

Overall, the examination addresses several key areas. Each general area, as conceptualized by the Association of State and Provincial Psychology Boards (formerly the American Association of State Psychology Boards), which sponsors the EPPP, is outlined below. It should be emphasized that the EPPP is continually revised and modified, that no two examinations are exactly the same, and that no two content areas are assessed in exactly the same way. Similarly, no two patients, although demonstrating similar psychiatric diagnoses, will present their symptoms in exactly the same way. The examination content, defined by the Association of State and Provincial Psychology Boards in 1990, includes the following topic areas:

Area 1: Professional Ethics. This area comprises approximately 16.5% of the EPPP.

Area 2: Problem Definition/Diagnosis. This area comprises approximately 26% of the EPPP and includes such areas as assessment, human development, psychopathology, motivation, intelligence, and psychopharmacology.

Area 3: Design, Implementation, and Assessment of Intervention. This area comprises approximately 26% of the EPPP and includes marriage and family therapy, community psychology, and crisis intervention.

Area 4: Research and Measurement. This area comprises approximately 17.5% of the EPPP.

Area 5: Applications to Social Systems. This area comprises the remaining 14% of the EPPP.

Candidates must demonstrate on the EPPP that they have a strong command of knowledge in the five areas. Because questions often blend situations involving examples that may bridge one, two, or more core areas of knowledge, it is in a candidate's best interest to comprehensively study all content areas.

Prepackaged review materials are useful for study in that key points of the EPPP are already highlighted. However, candidates who prepare their own study guides need not be at a disadvantage. The Association of State and Provincial Psychology Boards has study items available from previous examinations and can provide relevant study material.

Key Point to Remember: As you prepare for the licensing examination, be aware of the focus of your efforts. Too often candidates study what they already know, rather than what they need to know and do not know.

Candidates should keep a notecard, such as the sample below, that highlights specific examination topics and areas that need attention.

Plan Sufficient Preparatory Time

The Examination for Professional Practice in Psychology (EPPP) is designed to assess overall breadth of knowledge of applicants

Self-Assessment Exercise 4-1

List the general areas you believe will require the most study.

_____

_____

_____

Upon what do you base your thinking?

_____

_____

_____

Which areas do you dread studying? Why?

_____

_____

_____

for licensure or certification as psychologists from university programs and professional schools of psychology throughout the United States. Candidates are expected, in addition to the requisite doctoral degree, to have completed one or two years of post-doctoral training as well. In short, prerequisites are unusually strong and, given the diversity of training of applicants, it would be presumptuous to think that all candidates would come prepared with completely comparable training. One school may emphasize certain skills, other schools may highlight different

EXAMINATION STUDY GUIDE:
MAJOR AREAS OF FOCUS

NAME:_____

DATE: _____

DATE OF EXAMINATION: _____

EXAMINATION TOPICS:

__ Professional Ethics (Approximately 16.5%)

__ Problem Definition/Diagnosis (Approximately 26%)

__ Design, Implementation, and Assessment of Intervention (Approximately 26%)

__ Research and Measurement (Approximately 17.5%)

__ Applications to Social Systems (Approximately 14%)

areas of knowledge. Consequently, applicants are not equally knowledgeable in all areas.

If candidates need or wish to strengthen their knowledge in one or more core areas, it would be most beneficial to plan sufficient preparatory time for the task. Fortunately, psychology licensure requires postdoctoral training, affording candidates the opportunity to suitably prepare for the examination.

Most candidates can usefully consider beginning a preparatory study design approximately six to eight months before the examination. They should address the following points:

- Develop a study plan.
- Select study aids and materials.
- Locate a suitable study partner (if available).
- Secure an appropriate place to study.

For many candidates, getting started is a challenge. Many people procrastinate. If you delay starting, however, you will lose invaluable study time. By starting early, six to eight months before the examination, you can approach your goal in a realistic fashion. Sufficient preparatory time is key. Would you have attempted to take all your doctoral courses in one semester? Of course not. Likewise, it is important to plan and schedule a realistic amount of preparatory time to adequately and properly prepare for the licensure exam.

Key Point to Remember: No matter how good the study materials or how brilliant the candidate, one simply cannot

---

Self-Assessment Exercise 4-2

Review the amount of time you have considered allocating to study. Did you plan one week, one month, six months, or nine months to prepare for the examination?

_____

Did you plan sufficient time to adequately prepare?

_____

Did you consider attending a 5-day review workshop?

_____

How effectively designed is your schedule?

_____

_____

_____

learn without actually studying the materials one needs to learn. If there is one overall mistake unsuccessful candidates make, it is that they do not devote sufficient time to preparation. This is why it is so critical to plan sufficient preparatory time. Consider and plan your preparation carefully.

Use a Comprehensive Study Program

Studying previous exam questions or reading one of the available standardized review books is insufficient preparation for most candidates. In many ways, licensure is an opportunity to consolidate all the different facets of knowledge you studied while in graduate school. To maximize learning, candidates should:

- learn more than facts;
- strive to apply concepts to different situations;
- challenge themselves to understand the concepts;
- learn from mock examinations why a specific answer is correct and other answers are incorrect.

Choosing appropriate study materials is a difficult, often underrated task. To a large degree, your efforts will relate to the quality of material you use. Look over the material carefully. Look at the authors, the faculty giving workshops, and the success of the graduates. If possible, locate and secure feedback from previous candidates. Then, select what best will fit your individual needs. The following ten study strategies may be helpful:

1. attending a review course;
2. using audiotapes;
3. using a study system;
4. monitoring understanding;
5. emphasizing overlearning;
6. stressing organization;
7. maximizing concentration;
8. reinforcing successful learning;
9. developing a consistent study schedule;
10. using reviews and mock exams.

ATTEND A REVIEW COURSE.

Review courses, typically offered throughout the United States, can be enormously helpful. Even for well-qualified and prepared

Self-Assessment Exercise 4-3

Examine your study materials. What review program have you selected?

_____

_____

_____

What study materials will you use?

_____

_____

_____

licensure candidates, the opportunity to hear the information reviewed orally can be enormously useful. But, review courses can do much more than simply review: many actually teach you what you did not study as a student. For most candidates, an auditory presentation, added as an adjunct to book study, adds an important preparatory dimension. Furthermore, the inevitable questions and answers the workshops offer further enhance learning.

USING AUDIOTAPES.

Without qualification, audiotapes are a useful study aid for candidates. Fortunately, many of the commercially marketed review programs offer audiotapes to supplement written materials. These are excellent and can be used while jogging, driving, or performing household chores. Aside from the fact that audiotapes can provide a break from the monotonous nature of traditional textbook learning, an auditory support system adds a multisensory learning aid that is useful for many candidates.

USING A COHERENT STUDY SYSTEM.

Your study program should be complementary, with each part strengthening the others. A week-long review course, for instance, can be invaluable in teaching new material and in systematically reviewing overall exam parts in a structured and systematic way. However, it can be insufficient if used alone. So, too, can audiotapes, text materials, and/or review questions. Each of the parts—for example, a standardized review course, audiotape materials, text materials, and mock questions and answers—when used with the others, can contribute to a coherent system. Moreover, because of the overall diversity, boredom can be minimized.

Key Point to Remember: Your success will be reflective of the quality of material you select to guide your study. Whatever materials you ultimately choose, be sure that the preparatory materials you select or design are focused on each of the general areas assessed by the examination. Above all else, select those study aids best suited for *your* learning style and individual needs. Choose your curriculum wisely.

Monitor Your Understanding

One of the most challenging components to licensure involves the diverse ways different facets of knowledge are pieced together in the examination. Among other things, candidates must realize that it is vital to be able to apply concepts in a host of different situations. In addition, candidates must recognize certain underlying concepts and principles and fit different pieces of information together effectively. Study time should take this into account.

As you encounter different pieces of knowledge, it will be important to continually test and monitor understanding. Consider developing a notebook of points you will need to explore further. Also, the level of comprehension suggested here, certainly a challenging level, can be enhanced through participation in study groups, seminar participation, and the use of mock ex-

Self-Assessment Exercise 4-4

As you design your preparatory program, consider whether the study materials you plan to use are comprehensive. Are the materials clear and timely?

_____

_____

Have you addressed each of the examination content areas?

_____

_____

Can you supplement your review materials with classroom study?

_____

_____

If you are considering review classes, are faculty members licensed psychologists?

_____

_____

Are the classes small or large?

_____

Can you contact successful licensure candidates for feedback on the review course and/or study materials? Do you have their names and addresses?

_____

_____

Are the materials and your study plan comprehensive?

_____

Self-Assessment Exercise 4-5

Learning is enhanced when students apply and analyze what they learn. It is important, therefore, to realize when you are memorizing facts and when you have sufficient understanding to understand each concept thoroughly. As an example, simply knowing the definition of primary, secondary, and tertiary intervention is insufficient for passing the licensure examination. Can you provide examples of each?

_____

_____

_____

Likewise, can you correctly classify different treatment programs in each category?

_____

_____

_____

Test your knowledge. Where would you classify alcohol education?

_____

_____

_____

aminations that can tap knowledge areas in a variety of different ways. Decide whether you will be content, as a candidate for licensure or as a psychologist, to settle for less than the highest standards of knowledge and understanding.

Although most candidates strive to understand the science of psychology, there is a danger that candidates can mistake memorization of facts for understanding. This is one reason that many states supplement the multiple choice examination with essay and/or oral examination questions. Experience has shown, though, that, even in states without these components, there are candidates who will find the multiple choice examination more difficult than they imagined. Candidates who understand each question and each of the answer choices are in the strongest position to secure licensure. Systematic study, careful review, and periodic assessments that evaluate both knowledge and understanding can help.

Self-Assessment Exercise 4-6

Examine your study habits and self-examination tools. How will you assess your ability to apply new information to diverse situations?

_____

_____

List the strategies that you plan to use to help maximize understanding.

_____

_____

_____

Key Point to Remember: It is helpful if you design learning aids to maximize understanding, rather than rely on rote recall. The exam questions assess more than rote knowledge. You might also consider teaming with a study partner. Practice applying what you learn in diverse situations, and reason through distracting alternative possibilities.

Emphasize Overlearning

Licensure candidates are encouraged to emphasize overlearning in order to improve memory retrieval and accuracy of learning. In other words, overlearning allows one to recall information more easily and more accurately than information that is not overlearned. For licensure candidates, this is most helpful.

Licensure Preparatory Worksheet for Factual Questions

STUDY GROUP DESIGN FORMAT

Step 1. Select specific area of focus for session.

Step 2. Prepare questions and answers for study theme.

Step 3. Present questions to study partner.

Step 4. Have partner select answer and defend choices. Discuss incorrect choices.

Step 5. Make notes about areas of concern.

Independent Study Option:

> If a study partner is not available, solicit a helper who will present questions orally and monitor written answers. Observe strict timelines for questions and answers.

When candidates have overlearned information, it becomes less difficult to locate correct answers to multiple choice questions, and essay and oral examination questions are more easily addressed and resolved. Students are more comfortable in examination situations when they have a solid command of knowledge. The following study aids help to emphasize overlearning:

SUMMARIZE DAILY AND WEEKLY.

Summarizing offers an excellent opportunity to review, process, and overlearn information. It should be done at the end of each session and again weekly. Give proper time to summarizing; it may need to be complex. You should tailor summaries to your goal, framing your review summaries in terms of the types of questions you might encounter on the examination. As an example, if you have been studying Piagetian theory, use examples of different levels of reasoning, and see if you can correctly categorize each level into each developmental stage. Then, identify the type of reasoning representative of each stage.

HIGHLIGHT CRITICAL POINTS.

Highlighting can be helpful, if not overdone. Do not highlight every point. Instead, highlight essential points that can serve as central ideas around which you may be able to organize your thinking. You should develop a note system listing areas and times for review every week or month.

It helps to use two or three different colored highlighters as you study: a blue highlighter might indicate especially difficult areas you feel are most critical to learn; yellow might indicate areas of importance that are less perplexing intellectually. Develop a color system to enhance your learning and overlearning.

TURN MAIN POINTS INTO QUESTIONS.

The EPPP is a multiple choice, question-oriented examination. Therefore, it is to your advantage to use multiple choice questions for your own study: rephrase the different sections and subsections as questions and look for answers. By doing so, you can facilitate learning and memory retention.

Using the subject area of cognitive assessment (Area 2) as an example, ask yourself questions such as, what age cut offs are suggested for each of the Wechsler intelligence tests; what groups do you know that are better tested with the Stanford-Binet; and is it ethical to train a special education teacher or mental health worker to administer the tests. These questions may highlight areas that require further study. Most often, with one or two questions, you can identify areas of strength and weakness.

Keep Information Relevant.

Information is learned best when it seems relevant and meaningful. Likewise, retrieval and memory storage work best when new information is superimposed on existing knowledge. You should continually relate new information to what you know already.

In practice, see if you can relate new points to at least two pieces of existing knowledge. By associating new information with old, the new information will be retrieved more easily.

Key Point to Remember: Overlearning maximizes long-term retention and enhances accuracy of knowledge. Don't be content simply to study and review: Strive to overlearn.

Stress Organization

The importance of organization cannot be overstressed. Licensure candidates need to organize information to facilitate memory storage and retrieval. It is important to organize and structure the study process to provide unity in learning, and it is vital to design and select study materials that are well-organized and present information in a fashion that promotes learning and development. The ability to organize can be instrumental in the way you will store and learn new information.

Make Things Complementary.

If you study statistics and research methodology in the morning and jog in the afternoon, you might listen to your tape on statistics and research methodology while jogging. Study aids that complement each other help provide a unified, organized framework for learning.

Self-Assessment Exercise 4-7

How can you adapt existing study strategies to maximize over-learning?

_____

_____

Can you recall a time you overlearned information?

_____

_____

What do you need to do to overlearn?

_____

ORGANIZE STUDY AIDS.

Write note cards for each study activity, and keep the cards read-ily available so that you can refer to them while shopping, preparing dinner, or gardening. The better organized you are, the more easily your study efforts can become integrated into your life.

ASSESS YOUR ORGANIZATIONAL MAKEUP.

Everyone learns in different ways. Some people process informa-tion best in a quiet, subdued environment. Other people learn best in seeming total chaos. You should design an organizational format that works best for you. Try not to leave anything to chance; licensure is simply too important. An organized plan that addresses your individual needs can be an essential ingredi-ent to success.

Licensure Preparatory Summary Worksheet

STRENGTHS, WEAKNESSES, AND KEY POINTS:

_____

_____

_____

_____

KEY POINTS TO REVIEW:

_____

_____

_____

_____

PAGES TO REVIEW:

_____

_____

_____

_____

QUESTIONS TO INVESTIGATE:

_____

_____

_____

_____

Licensure candidates may find the following organization strategies helpful:

- Organize similar points together.
- Organize new information into meaningful wholes.
- Organize new information around existing knowledge.
- Organize study aids (notecards) for overlearning.

Organizational skills do not always come easily to everyone, no matter how intelligent or well-educated the person. Therefore, it is necessary for many people to put more effort into this area than others. It is part of the nature of things. In generating and developing your preparatory plan, you should examine your own organizational strengths and weaknesses. In the following paragraph, several questions are posed to help pinpoint organizational strengths and weaknesses. After you conduct the self-examination, you should realize that the introspective process only assumes meaning if you design productive strategies that can openly and successfully deal with the need for organization to achieve licensure.

Key Point to Remember: In practice, organizational weaknesses often can become glaring when the need arises for self-organized learning. Licensure candidates need to realize the important role organization plays in studying effectively.

In fact, organization can serve as a unifying framework for licensure. Therefore, candidates should design a preparatory plan that organizes similar points together, new information into meaningful wholes, new information around existing knowledge, and study aids (such as note cards) into a format for overlearning.

Maximize Concentration

Concentration is something educators speak of often. Yet, it seems nebulous. Without due concentration, you are not likely to process all you need to learn. However, there are strategies you can use to maximize your concentration.

SELECT A PEACEFUL STUDY AREA.

Most individuals find excessive noise distracting. For example, studying in a busy living room, with children playing nearby,

Self-Assessment Exercise 4-8

Like most people, psychologists are organized in some situations and disorganized in others. Identify three different occasions when you have been well-organized.

_____

_____

_____

Likewise, identify three occasions when you seemed completely in disarray.

_____

_____

_____

Which occasions felt better?

_____

_____

Using the occasions listed above as examples, identify your organizational strengths.

_____

_____

_____

Identify your organizational weaknesses.

_____

_____

_____

Use the list you developed above as a framework to design an effective preparatory study program.

Licensure Organizational Worksheet

PLANNED STUDY PROGRAM

GENERAL GOAL:

_____

_____

_____

_____

SPECIFIC QUESTIONS:

_____

_____

_____

STUDY POINTS: (SUN., MON., TUES., WED., THUR., FRI., SAT.)

_____

_____

_____

_____

_____

_____

_____

would be excessively distracting for most people. A study area free of distraction is usually best.

Whatever your choice for a study location, you should realize that loud noises or ongoing distraction of other students, friends, children, or family can minimize your concentration. Select a study space that best fits your needs. If this is at home, solicit support from your family or housemates. Perhaps a house rule can be established for quiet time during certain designated hours.

MINIMIZE EMOTIONAL DISTRACTIONS.

People often cannot concentrate when key emotional factors are exerting pressure. Unfortunately, life sometimes cannot be controlled and structured as we might desire. After all, the world is not perfect. Psychologists know this better than most people. Nevertheless, certain distractions can be minimized. For example, it would not be a good idea to move from one home or apartment to another while preparing for the licensing examination.

Self-Assessment Exercise 4-9

Can you study best at home, or in a local university or library study cubicle?

_____

Where did you study best while you were a student?

_____

Where do you plan to study for licensure?

_____

_____

Sometimes, of course, such events cannot be avoided. Whenever possible, however, you should consider the implications of major lifestyle changes while preparing for the licensing examination and strive to minimize distractions.

MAINTAIN A HEALTHY LIFESTYLE.

Regardless of one's intellectual abilities, one thing is clear: people cannot perform at their peak when they are exhausted, malnourished, or physically rundown. Many students ignore this important ingredient to success. It is important to sleep, eat nourishing meals, and exercise at least moderately. A healthy lifestyle maximizes energy, keeps the mind clear and rested, and helps establish a healthful atmosphere for learning.

USE MOCK QUESTIONS TO FOCUS ATTENTION.

Teachers know that in-class questioning can quickly focus student attention. You should consider using the same strategy in your study sessions. Practice questions can be useful tools to help maximize concentration and focus, particularly when they are focused on study material you are developing and are complemented by a study style that continually offers opportunities to turn textual material into questions.

Obviously, attention is a complex variable. However, by keeping your study material varied, by minimizing excessive noise and disrupting influences, and by utilizing a study system that uses questions as an ongoing way to focus attention, you can establish a study plan that will help maximize your learning.

Key Point to Remember: Students who are able to concentrate can maximize study time. Although it sometimes seems impossible, not everyone needs complete silence to concentrate and learn. Some students, in fact, seem able to concentrate in the midst of what might seem total pandemonium to another person. Not everyone, though, can claim this ability. Without concentration, learning is simply not going to progress in an efficient way. Study times and places should be selected when and where you can concentrate most effectively.

Self-Assessment Exercise 4-10

Identify factors that detract from your concentration and study efforts.

_____

_____

_____

_____

At what times of the day can you concentrate most effectively?

_____

What is it about these times that enables you to concentrate effectively?

_____

_____

_____

List ways you can maximize concentration while preparing for licensure.

_____

_____

_____

_____

Reinforce Successful Learning

Licensure candidates should understand that they are likely to experience feelings of general complacency from time to time. Fortunately, learning to plan personal rewards can be a strong ally in helping to maintain a strong dedication for the task at hand.

According to behavioral psychology, behaviors that are followed by rewards, or satisfiers, are more likely to be repeated or learned. In a similar fashion, it is useful to reinforce learning while preparing for licensure.

Rewards can help stimulate learning. First, however, reinforcers must be designed and accepted in correct ways. This means, for example, that reinforcers must follow the correct response: studying. Unfortunately, too many students take their rewards first, and then they excuse themselves from study. Follow what you know (or will know as you study operant conditioning) to reinforce your own learning.

Ideally, one learns for the internal sense of accomplishment, as well as for the ultimate reward, in this case, licensure. Pairing a reward with some behavior, like studying, can increase the likelihood of repeating that behavior and simultaneously make that behavior seem more pleasurable. By planning certain rewards—perhaps a movie, a special dinner, or a two-day holiday—learning can take on new meaning. In fact, it can even begin to act as a motivator.

What happens when you receive a reinforcer too late? Usually, people find it irritating. If possible, plan your own rewards and reinforcers to follow your efforts immediately. As an illustration, plan a special dinner or outing after you complete your first mock examination. Choose a favorite activity, but make it contingent on completing the mock examination. In this way, you can begin to associate something you enjoy doing with something you likely won't completely enjoy doing. (Educational psychologists, incidently, refer to this as the Premack principle. David Premack learned that people will perform some behavior if doing that particular behavior allows or enables them to complete another behavior.)

As you select reinforcers, choose ones that are meaningful and pleasurable to you. Often, people choose or are given reinforcers that others deem appropriate. As an illustration, I remember that as a youngster in elementary school, I was offered the choice of several reinforcers for completing certain reading assignments during summer vacation. One summer I thought a slingshot would be great. Usually, though, I asked for a selection of pleasure books and comic books. I imagine other children might have shunned any additional reading, but I saw a great difference between mythological tales, which I adored, and the reading lists that the library suggested. Fortunately, my parents knew it was my choice. You should choose reinforcers *you* will find reinforcing.

Key Point to Remember: Positive reinforcers can serve as useful enhancements for study. In fact, reinforcers that follow certain behaviors, such as studying, can increase the frequency of that behavior. That is the basic tenet behind operant conditioning. As psychologists, candidates should appreciate the important role reinforcers can have in behavior. Don't wait until you are frustrated; plan rewards for your study.

Develop a Consistent Study Schedule

Consistency is a critical element in any successful preparation program. Slow and steady does pave the way. Admittedly, there has been some psychometric criticism of programs that claim to increase test scores. Yet, a consistent and long-term preparation program, one that resembles a true educational experience by developing knowledge over a long time span rather than through cramming, throws a damper on those who chide preparatory programs.

A consistent study program has several advantages. For example, it offers the potential for enormous learning. In fact, consistent study would be comparable to regular practice sessions by a musician. In music, of course, distributed practice is preferred over massed practice. Similar statements are true for learning in psychology. Consistency is the key to a routinized study program.

Another advantage of consistent study is that it offers opportunities for continuous reinforcement paradigms. Individuals who are reinforced consistently (if you remember your lessons in behavioral psychology) learn more rapidly than those who are reinforced inconsistently.

You may hear or learn that some candidates prefer to study only on weekends, or they will do nothing but study for

Self-Assessment Exercise 4-11

Consider what reinforcers you might use during your study sessions. List three favorite activities you might select.

_____

_____

_____

What reinforcers might be used after reviewing statistics?

_____

_____

Identify reinforcers you might use to reinforce your spouse, best friend, housemate, lover, or roommate for helping during your EPPP preparation.

_____

_____

_____

_____

How will you react when you skip, cancel, or otherwise ignore a planned study session? Will you still sample the reward?

_____

How would a behavioral psychologist handle the problem?

_____

_____

the last two weeks prior to the examination. This is not ideal, because cramming does not allow proper time for overlearning, and massed study blocks do not offer sufficient opportunities for rehearsal and elaboration. Consistent study efforts, on the other hand, can offer the potential to learn more material, to learn new material, to elaborate and process information, and to extend learning to a point where mastery learning is achieved.

Key Point to Remember: Consistency is an indispensable study aid. In particular, a study framework that fosters consistent, applied, comprehensive, and integrated efforts can make a major difference in preparation and outcome. Alternatively, inconsistent, halfhearted efforts can spell failure.

Self-Assessment Exercise 4-12

How consistently did you study while you were a graduate student? Did you wait to study until final exams? Or, did you move along in a consistent fashion? Review and write down the patterns you have seen over the past few years. List occasions in which you were most consistent.

_____

_____

_____

_____

Did you need someone to provide a helpful nudge (or shove)?

_____

Use Reviews and Mock Examinations

Periodic reviews and the use of mock examination testing can play crucial roles in helping candidates assess learning and identify areas of weakness. Moreover, periodic review periods reinforce overlearning and offer the opportunity to relate new information with existing knowledge. Use mock examinations to provide important test simulations that focus the learner on the examination format.

As noted previously, some candidates avoid review periods or skim through review periods without expending the energy necessary to the task. Likewise, other candidates neglect general learning and simply study and memorize answers to mock examination questions. Neither approach is ideal.

Individuals who memorize examination questions and answers, or do not thoroughly learn important material through overlearning and rehearsal, risk trouble. Examination questions, by design, can assess key points in an infinite number of different ways. Because questions can be formulated in complex and divergent ways, it is important that candidates be able to understand the information fully in order to avoid distractors and alternative answers. This is why elaboration is stressed. Candidates who are able to apply concepts to a host of situations are far better prepared than those who only know one example for a given problem.

Ongoing review blocks and mock examinations can form a foundation for licensure. To realize their full potential, though, it is helpful to use the concepts in an active, positive way. For example, you could take one of the mock examinations as if it was the actual licensure examination. Dress as you might on the day of the actual examination. Take the mock examination in an unfamiliar location. Time it, and then grade and score your performance.

Carefully chart and address each area of weakness you identify. Key study issues can differ for each candidate. A Ph.D. from the California School of Professional Psychology who pursued specialty training in neuropsychology, for example, probably will not require the same study time on neuropsychology and physiological psychology as might a candidate who lacks such specialty training. In the same vein, a Psy.D. in school psychology from New York University most likely will possess a strong foundation of knowledge on psychometric theory and intellectual assessment. However, both candidates may profit from careful study of industrial and organizational psychology.

Ongoing review sessions can reinforce new learning and mock examinations can assess strengths and weaknesses. Use mock examinations to your best advantage: Do more than simply memorize correct answers. Study why each answer is correct and why certain options are incorrect. Rephrase questions and use the results to assess your knowledge.

Self-Assessment Exercise 4-13

What do you think you can learn from continuing review and mock examinations in your preparation for licensure?

_____

_____

_____

How have you approached such opportunities historically?

_____

_____

_____

What (if anything) will you need to change in your thinking in order to maximize these opportunities?

_____

_____

_____

Key Point to Remember: Periodic review sessions and mock examinations are effective and useful study aids. They can pinpoint specific weaknesses and highlight areas of weakness, which you can target for study. Also, it is important to analyze why, on mock examinations, each alternative is incorrect. Understand the rationale behind selecting the correct answer and, in this way, go beyond memorization of facts.

CONCLUSIONS

In developing an effective preparatory study program, licensure candidates may focus on several key points that can enhance learning. This chapter explored ten study strategies that can be used as focal points for learning. You may wish to review these strategies and consider how they can be used to enhance your efforts. The ten study strategies are:

1. Study pertinent pieces of information.
2. Plan sufficient preparatory time.
3. Use a comprehensive study program.
4. Monitor your understanding.
5. Emphasize overlearning.
6. Stress organization.
7. Maximize concentration.
8. Reinforce successful learning.
9. Develop a consistent study schedule.
10. Use ongoing reviews and mock examinations.

Licensure is a challenging task. Think back and consider whether previous challenges you addressed might have been more effectively handled by designing your learning as discussed in this chapter. After you consider these points, remember that you need use only those elements that can effectively enhance your learning. Take what is useful and discard the rest.

Self-Assessment Exercise 4-14

Consider how you can apply each of the above strategies to your schedule. Is your learning well-organized?

_____

Are you blending both mock questions and ongoing review with textbook learning?

_____

Are you utilizing audio tapes in order to maximize auditory input?

_____

Are you studying on a regular basis?

_____

Are you rewarding your efforts?

_____

5 Preparation for Oral Examination

Chapter Preview

WHAT CAN YOU DO TO PREPARE FOR ORAL EXAMINATION?

PURPOSE

Oral examinations can sometimes seem Herculean. Like the Examination for Professional Practice in Psychology (EPPP), the oral examination can tap a range of knowledge. With careful study, however, licensure candidates can reflect both strong communication and clinical skills.

STRATEGY

Specific study strategies for licensure can:

- focus self-appraisal efforts;
- provide anticipatory planning;
- monitor mock simulations;
- guide study efforts and progress;
- maintain a positive orientation.

ORAL EXAMINATION REQUIREMENTS

The oral examination is an important supplement to the Examination for Professional Practice in Psychology (EPPP), used by approximately 70% of the psychology boards in the United States. Fortunately, in a number of respects, you can relax somewhat. Many of the preparatory strategies outlined in preceding chapters will be helpful in preparing for the oral examination. In

Self-Assessment Exercise 5-1

What are your feelings regarding your comfort level with oral examinations?

_____

_____

Are you familiar with the content areas that the Board of Psychology suggests are likely topics for oral examination?

_____

Do you intend to become part of a study group?

_____

Do you plan to locate a study partner with whom you can refine your oral examination skills?

_____

Does your study plan address the oral examination as well as the EPPP?

_____

fact, candidates who take advantage of the benefits that can be accrued from working with a study partner or in a study group are in a particularly strong position.

Oral examinations demand expressive (communication) skills and organizational skills not necessarily required (at least, not in the same way) in objective multiple-choice examinations. The latter require that candidates choose the correct answer from a selection of answers. Oral examinations, on the other hand, require that candidates formulate the correct answer in their minds and then orally, in front of a panel, present verbal arguments and conceptualizations.

Critics of oral examinations cite the effect that anxiety and poise can have on examiner bias. Unquestionably, oral examinations demand verbal and relational skills. Whatever the criticisms, however, if the oral examination is required in the state in which you intend to become licensed, do not spend too much time highlighting your criticisms and biases. Prepare for the exam.

Self-Assessment Exercise 5-2

Are you comfortable speaking in front of a panel?

_____

How do you react to confrontational questions?

_____

How do you react when you feel confused during interviews?

_____

Are you comfortable speaking orally about professional issues?

_____

PREPARATION STRATEGIES

Candidates should honestly assess their individual strengths and weaknesses. Obviously, the licensure oral examination is rigorous. Many people find oral presentations, graded or otherwise, intimidating. However, candidates should be encouraged by the fact that they have answered many oral questions in countless lectures, discussions, and seminars while they were graduate students.

There are many possible formats that can be utilized for oral examinations. Most licensure candidates have actually participated in many oral examination situations, often identified by other terminology. For example, classroom presentations, from high school to graduate school, are, in fact, oral examinations. A doctoral dissertation defense is another type of oral examination. Most likely, you have already successfully completed numerous oral examinations.

Key Point to Remember: One ingredient of successful preparation for oral examinations is an initial honest and realistic self-appraisal. Take stock of your skills in this area. Consider composition, organization, presentation, structure, coherence, and cognitive retrieval. Successful candidates know their strengths as well as their weaknesses. Oral examinations are passable.

Anticipate Examination Topics

Although individual examination questions differ from one examination to the next, it is appropriate to consider the areas typically assessed: Does the oral examination generally address state law or professional ethics, or are the examination topics drawn from broad areas of professional practice?

Although examination security cannot (and certainly should not) be abridged, state psychology boards sometimes will provide candidates with general information on areas to be covered. For example, California, which utilizes an oral examination in conjunction with the EPPP, notifies applicants of areas to be covered in the oral examination and only examines candidates in those areas.*

---

* State of California, Psychology Licensing Law, Section 1388.5: Oral Examinations, 1990.

Self-Assessment Exercise 5-3

Identify three different times you participated in oral presentations and were successful. If you can't think of examples, remember that English and drama classes use oral presentations regularly as an evaluation format.

_____

_____

_____

What specific aspect of communication hinders your best performance on oral presentations? Consider such things as anxiety, presentation, structure, organization, and form.

_____

_____

_____

How have you approached oral presentations in the past? What strategies did you utilize?

_____

_____

_____

How did you approach graded presentations or seminar participation as a doctoral student?

_____

_____

List two times you were successful.

_____

_____

It can be helpful to focus your study strategies on specific areas targeted in the oral examination. Review your state licensure application materials for specific information that may be germane to your needs, and be particularly conscious of any information highlighted by the licensure board.

Key Point to Remember: It is particularly important to explore potential topics that may be tested on the oral examination. Go through the licensure regulations and application materials carefully. Speak to past candidates. Then, compile a list of questions you might utilize as a beginning outline for study. If possible, structure your study sessions in a format similar to the actual examination procedure.

Conduct Simulated Oral Examinations

Virtually any behavior can be refined or changed, according to the principles of operant conditioning. Oral examination skills can also be refined, changed, and enhanced. This section will review selected study strategies designed to do exactly that.

Practice examinations that are designed to approximate the actual oral examination can be most instructive. For example, licensure candidates initially may utilize a study group structured to resemble the oral examination board. Participants can role play and question candidates in a similar fashion. More frequently rehearsed information is remembered more easily than information that is practiced infrequently.

Using successive approximation strategies, candidates might gradually structure practice sessions to increasingly resemble the licensure examination itself. This might include having all participants dress like the actual oral board. Likewise, by using different study partners, candidates can reduce their apprehension regarding different examination teams. If candidates are completing their postdoctoral training in a hospital, a clinic, or a facility with several senior staff, it may be possible to solicit the participation of the senior psychologists. This can make the learning situation more meaningful and provide an organizational structure in which different perspectives and presentation styles can be experienced.

Even with this, the oral examination can bring a sense of the unexpected that can be disconcerting to candidates. An unex-

Self-Assessment Exercise 5-4

What are specific content areas you need to strengthen prior to the oral examination?

_____

_____

_____

_____

_____

_____

What specific questions could pose difficulty?

_____

_____

_____

In what areas are you strong?

_____

_____

_____

In what areas do you need further study?

_____

_____

pected topic, an unusual perspective or inquiry, or a scowling facial expression from an examiner can often serve as a barrier to success. Therefore, as you refine your oral examination skills, consider what would most disturb your sense of comfort. Then, have colleagues or study partners assist you with these problems.

Key Point to Remember: It is important both to review and learn examination topics and to become familiar with the examination format used by the licensing board. Familiarity with oral examination procedures can reduce anxiety and enhance self-assurance. One of the best ways to become comfortable is through practice sessions designed to closely approximate or simulate the actual examination itself. Practice simulated oral examinations with partners.

Monitor Your Progress

One ingredient for success on oral examinations involves self-confidence. Obviously, the possibility always exists that an

---

Self-Assessment Exercise 5-5

What would most rattle you in the examination? Would it be a specific question? An examiner's demeanor? Write down specific examples of problems and situations that concern you.

_____

_____

_____

_____

_____

examiner may make an unexpected inquiry that takes the candidate completely by surprise. It happens. Still, this plight can befall all candidates. Obviously, though, preparation should enhance self-confidence. One useful strategy to assist preparation for the oral examination is to use a self-monitoring system to measure your progress.

Consider a videotape or an audiotape. You may also find it useful to have a study partner assume the role of an impartial observer during oral examination simulations. Much as a clinical supervisor might observe a group or family therapy session through a one-way mirror and provide a fresh perspective, so, too, a study partner in the role of a monitor or observer can provide a useful perspective.

Key Point to Remember: Assessment and evaluation is a hallmark for psychologists. Similarly, candidates can benefit from a certain amount of self-introspection and examination. Explore the benefits that you might accrue through the use of a monitoring system. Videotape and audiotape systems and independent observers all can be useful.

Maintain a Positive Attitude

Psychological mental health is simply too important to ignore. Licensure candidates need a healthy positive attitude. One of the best advantages of having a positive attitude is that you can enhance motivation and effort. A positive attitude also can help maintain study momentum so that you continue to study with diligence and persistence.

Usually there are a number of ingredients involved in fostering and maintaining a positive attitude. Likewise, there are numerous reasons why candidates can have a defeatist, negative attitude. Obviously, a negative orientation is not going to motivate learning and development. Usually, negativity breeds negativity. Because the oral examination affords examiners the opportunity to individually meet and evaluate licensure candidates on an interpersonal level, a negative attitude can become quickly apparent. After all, the examiners are trained to detect and analyze personality dynamics. Therefore, in designing and executing a preparatory program for licensure, it is helpful to consider your attitude.

Self-Assessment Exercise 5-6

What three strengths do you think you can bring to the oral examination?

_____

_____

_____

What three strengths of yours do your study partners identify?

_____

_____

_____

What three weaknesses?

_____

_____

_____

Picture the worse-case scenario while you are actually taking the oral examination. What happened? Write a description of those areas you believe are impediments to your successfully passing the oral examination.

_____

_____

_____

Self-Assessment Exercise 5-7

How is your outlook? What tells you whether your attitude is positive or negative?

_____

_____

Can you identify emotions you associate with positive and negative days?

_____

What can you do to maintain a positive attitude? Do exercise and diet help?

_____

Will you need to change anything in order to foster or maintain positive orientation?

_____

_____

Key Point to Remember: A positive attitude can be a critical ingredient in a successful study program. Unfortunately, a negative outlook can destroy concentration, undermine motivation, and reduce energy. Licensure candidates should strive to maintain a positive attitude. A careful and well-designed study program is one key, as it can help provide a structured study format. Exercise and diet can help too. Overall, a positive attitude and the ingredients to maintain it should not be treated lightly. A positive outlook can fortify study efforts.

CONCLUSIONS

The regulatory body in each state that utilizes an oral examination as adjunct to the national Examination for Professional Practice in Psychology is aware that oral examinations provide a personal first-hand look at licensure candidates in psychology. This is no less true in California or Washington than in Ohio, Virginia, Texas, or New Jersey. How comfortable and experienced are you during an oral examination? Do you feel tense or emotional at the prospect of an oral examination?

In this chapter, we examined selected strategies that can be utilized to help prepare for the oral examination. Examine your oral examination skills. Look broadly at your individual strengths and weaknesses. Consider utilizing friends, co-workers, fellow candidates, and colleagues to help you prepare for this phase of the examination.

Consider utilizing a videotape or audiotape during study sessions. If possible, use peers and colleagues as mock examiners. Analyze your own answers and behaviors and request feedback from your study partners. Review the following strategies discussed in this chapter:

1. Conduct honest self-appraisals.
2. Anticipate examination topics.
3. Conduct simulated oral examinations.
4. Monitor progress.
5. Maintain a positive attitude.

Candidates should remember that oral examinations, overall, emphasize far more than learning specific facts. Certainly this is important, but oral examinations also give examiners the opportunity to observe candidates' interpersonal skills, cognitive reasoning, flexibility, and tact, as well as many of the psychological and psychosocial skills that are critical for the professional practice of psychology.

It is natural to feel tense during an oral examination. Fortunately, a study program that affords continual opportunities to practice and refine oral examination skills can be helpful to candidates. Candidates who address their weaknesses and who systematically work to effectively transfer what they know from study sessions into successively closer approximations of an actual examination should benefit.

6 Preparation for Essay Examination

Chapter Preview

HOW CAN THE ESSAY EXAMINATION BE APPROACHED CRITICALLY?

PURPOSE

Essay examinations encourage written organizational talents. Licensure candidates need to know specific facts and be able to present cogent summarizations.

STRATEGY

Study for the essay examination can:

- clarify specific and shifting areas of practice;
- help amplify alternative interpretations;
- refine organization of knowledge;
- focus attention on key facts, words, and ideas;
- establish a workable pace for examination.

ESSAY EXAMINATION REQUIREMENTS

The comparative merits of essay, multiple-choice, and oral examinations have been debated for many years among numerous groups and examination boards. Despite the widespread acceptance of the EPPP and the increasing use of multiple-choice examinations, essay exams are used by many state boards for licensure for professional practice in psychology.

The essay examination requires the ability to think clearly, to organize pertinent points, and to write in a clear fashion. Whereas the multiple-choice examination allows candidates the opportunity to select correct answers from a selection of choices, the essay examination affords the opportunity for the board of examiners to see each candidate's individual command of the subject matter, and it affords the opportunity for candidates to reveal their individual strengths and weaknesses. Essay questions assess a candidate's ability to analyze, organize, and canvass particular issues.

Assuredly, there are objections and criticisms about essay examinations. These largely involve the fact that candidates with superior English composition skills and the most legible prose may stand in a stronger position from which to achieve a high passing score. Most objectors believe that essay examinations offer too large an opportunity for grading variations.

Largely for these reasons, the essay examination increasingly has fallen into disuse. Further, in the states where it is still in use, it is never the sole criterion for licensure. It accompanies other examination procedures.

To ensure against inconsequential study efforts, candidates should consider designing a portion of their study program to the essay examination. Fortuitously, the preparatory strategies utilized in preparation for the Examination for Professional Practice in Psychology (EPPP) offer an overall orientation and depth of knowledge that can supplement specific essay examination preparatory efforts.

Putting aside criticisms concerning the reliability and validity of essay examinations, candidates should consider the reality of the examination itself and consider how to develop a workable study program.

Self-Assessment Exercise 6-1

What have you heard about the essay examination?

_____

_____

Are you comfortable summarizing psychological theories and bridging theory with practice?

_____

How well did you perform on essay examinations during graduate school? List three strengths.

_____

_____

_____

List three weaknesses.

_____

_____

_____

Preparation Strategies

To maximize study effectiveness, it can be most beneficial to try to one's best ability to anticipate general topical areas. Although general areas of focus, such as state jurisprudence or professional ethics, often can be anticipated, candidates should recognize that, as a general rule, actual questions are modified from one examination to the next.

SHIFTING PARAMETERS OF PRACTICE.

Candidates should be aware that prior topics may have different answers, as laws, professional ethical guidelines, and new research findings continually refine and change the overall parameters in which psychologists practice.

Key Point to Remember: For the practice of psychology, we need to be aware of the many changing complexities that can deeply affect each clinician, client, and organization. It is obvious there are important legal issues and ethical guidelines for practice that have been refined and modified. In addition, several psychological tests have been updated. Thus, candidates should be clear on the changing parameters of practice. These issues, particularly if they affect individual state regulations, are fair game for the essay examination. Anticipate essay questions by staying current.

ALTERNATIVE INTERPRETATIONS.

Whereas multiple-choice tests are designed so that candidates should conceivably recognize and select the best and most logical answer, essay examinations offer considerably more latitude. This can prove both good and bad.

Candidates should systematically consider, while preparing for the examination, different alternatives and learn why certain options are incorrect. Practically, this can be done to a large degree by analyzing why certain answers are incorrect on mock multiple choice examinations. This is a situation in which carry-over can occur from preparation for one examination to another.

Group study sessions also can be of use, as candidates can have the opportunity to hear feedback from other candidates and to subsequently acquire solutions that other candidates might feel are more appropriate. Although such presentations differ somewhat from essay examinations, there are many benefits to such an approach.

Key Point to Remember: In professional psychology, there are numerous areas of disagreement, as well as guidelines

Self-Assessment Exercise 6-2

Have you carefully scrutinized the examination application materials for general topical guidelines that might suggest areas for study? What are they?

_____

_____

_____

Have you been told, through either the board of psychology or other relevant sources, possible areas of examination focus? What are they?

_____

_____

_____

Do state laws or ethics routinely appear on the essay examination?

_____

How have you used written expressive skills recently?

_____

_____

How prepared are you at this moment for an essay exam? What more do you need to do?

_____

_____

_____

Self-Assessment Exercise 6-3

What are the different treatment modalities that can be used successfully with a patient in psychotherapy? Indeed, how effective is psychotherapy according to the literature? Outline your answer.

_____

_____

_____

_____

_____

Self-Assessment Exercise 6-4

What approaches have been used successfully with problem drinkers? Consider contrasting interpretations and outline your answer.

_____

_____

_____

_____

_____

Self-Assessment Exercise 6-5

Referring to the questions in exercises 6-3 and 6-4, how effectively can you compare and contrast differing points of view?

_____

_____

_____

What topics might be areas of assessment on the essay examination which will contain conflicting opinions?

_____

_____

_____

_____

_____

that can easily solicit multiple perspectives. Needless to say, essay examinations are particularly vulnerable to alternative interpretations and solutions. Clearly, candidates who are able to compare and contrast, clearly and succinctly, different opinions are in a strong position. Realize the challenge of presenting alternative positions.

PREPARING ORGANIZED INTERPRETATIONS.

The importance of organization cannot be overstressed when preparing an essay. As might be anticipated, well-organized answers convey a sense of clear and logical thinking. Also, a well-organized essay offers candidates the opportunity to clearly highlight key points and facts.

Organization is a key to problem solving. Remember how Sultan, the chimpanzee, provided Gestalt psychologists with critical cues to problem solving? Sitting inside his cage, Sultan was presented with an assortment of fruit, all just beyond his reach. At this point, Sultan might have given up. Fortunately, there was a solution: Two sticks were near Sultan, a short stick just inside the cage that was too short to reach the fruit and a longer stick outside the cage, also just beyond his reach but closer than the fruit.

After unsuccessfully trying to reach the fruit, Sultan picked up the shorter stick and with it pulled the longer stick to his cage. Then, with the longer stick, he was able to reach the fruit.

Of course, all this is open to interpretation. In fact, this interpretation largely reflects the way the information was organized. In any event, without organization, Sultan would not have received his reward and this section would not have been written.

How will you, as a licensure candidate, approach essay problems? In an organized fashion, or with disorganized chaos? The point is clear: consider the importance that organization can have in constructing a coherent interpretation for an essay problem.

Key Point to Remember: Essay examinations truly assess a candidate's organizational abilities. Within time limits, essay questions often assess areas that can involve a large body of published opinions. Therefore, candidates need to clearly organize their presentation. Short preparatory outlines are one strategy. These can include brief notes on key points. Short targeted paragraphs are another tool. Consider reviewing organizational strategies that you would find helpful. Then, ask for feedback from colleagues and peers. Don't leave organization to chance; plan your approach.

ATTENTION TO KEY WORDS.

Essay questions, like multiple-choice questions, often have one or two key words that can be critical to identifying the correct answers. As such, it is important to read essay questions care-

Self-Assessment Exercise 6-6

Consider the ways you can best organize essays. Would an outline be helpful and can it ultimately save time?

_____

_____

_____

Should you organize each paragraph around a main point?

_____

How will you present supportive concepts?

_____

_____

_____

How will you present your rationale?

_____

_____

List the strategies you plan to use on the exam.

_____

_____

_____

_____

fully. Be alert to words such as "clarify," "interpret," "contrast," or "compare." Each means something different.

What does "clarify" mean to you? When a question asks for "contrasting" opinions, do you stress similarities or differences? Hopefully, the latter. When a question requires a discussion or elaboration, do you present one side or two sides of a situation? In other words, would you examine the issue completely, presenting both pros and cons? Ideally, a discussion examines a problem thoroughly, exploring all sides of an issue.

Success on an essay examination involves understanding the question. Before writing an essay answer, carefully read the essay question to be sure of the specific slant being requested.

Key Point to Remember: Essay questions often evoke different responses from different candidates. Carefully read the essay question. Be attentive to key words. Be aware that it may be wiser to expend a few more minutes carefully reading the question than to design an inaccurate, misdirected answer. Understand exactly what the question asks.

ESTABLISHING A SOUND PACE.

Whether facing 200 multiple-choice questions on the EPPP or a series of essay examinations, candidates will find it useful to become skilled at pacing their answers. One of the best ways to practice and establish a workable examination pace is through practice examinations. After several simulated examination sessions, you should begin to sense how much time is necessary to correctly answer a series of essay questions. Simulated sessions help establish a realistic pace.

Pacing can involve several different ingredients. Everyone has different needs: One person may find it helpful to take a 5- or 10-minute break after each question; another may find a small snack between, or during, questions helpful. A solid exam strategy is to design a time frame that is comfortable for you. Consider taking short rest breaks. Also consider breaking a series of questions into several small examination units. Remember that the general idea is to establish a pace that effectively meets your needs.

Key Point to Remember: It is not difficult to approach examinations in a haphazard, seat-of-the-pants fashion. Some peo-

Self-Assessment Exercise 6-7

Can you recall times when you did not accurately address the question asked while taking an essay examination?

_____

_____

Were you ever in error not because you lacked sufficient knowledge to answer correctly but because you misunderstood the question?

_____

_____

What strategies have you utilized since that time to avoid such catastrophes?

_____

_____

_____

ple work full tilt until they have completed every question. They approach the examination as if it were a sprint. Other candidates, though, find it helpful to develop a more relaxed, modulated pace. Decide which approach is best for you. If you decide to develop a systematic self-paced approach, consider breaking the examination into several miniexams. Also, decide if several small rest breaks or one longer break would help maximize attention and concentration. Practice your strategies during simulated examinations.

Self-Assessment Exercise 6-8

Examine your test taking skills. Do you pace yourself well?

_____

Do you allot sufficient time to answer essay questions?

_____

How do you establish a sound pace?

_____

How much time do you plan to allow for outlining each essay response?

_____

_____

Have you considered general time boundaries for the essay examination?

_____

CONCLUSIONS

Essay examinations offer candidates the opportunity to reveal individual excellencies and to reflect reasoning and organizational abilities. Simultaneously, skills in English composition, general facility with the language, and legibility certainly cannot be discounted. In fact, it is due to the very effect such matters can have that essay examinations are often criticized.

In spite of previous and existing criticisms, however, essay examinations remain in use. Therefore, candidates undergoing licensure procedures in areas where the essay examination is required would do well to consider apportioning part of their time to preparation for this portion of the examination. After all, to ignore even one section of the examination is risky.

Five study designs to help prepare for essay examinations were explored in this chapter:

1. Remain aware of shifting parameters of practice.
2. Be aware of alternative interpretations.
3. Prepare organized interpretations.
4. Be attentive to key words.
5. Establish a sound pace.

Because no single preparatory strategy can be cited as clearly more superior, more desirous, or more important than any other, candidates desiring to improve their overall essay examination skills should consider each of the strategies in turn. In addition, it may be beneficial to review the chapter on preparatory strategies for the oral examination, as many of the points emphasized as useful for oral examinations can have value for essay examinations.

In any event, it is important to recognize the fact that, as with many test situations, essay examinations involve more than simply regurgitating facts and information. Successful candidates will need to organize, synthesize, and present facts, of course, but they also will need to assimilate information and present arguments in a logical fashion.

How refined are your essay examination skills? Have you considered your strengths and weaknesses? Have you designed a study program to enhance those skills that need to be strengthened? You need to design a study program that can best refine your skills.

7 Reflections and Projections

Chapter Preview

HOW CAN I REFLECTIVELY CONSIDER LICENSURE?

PURPOSE

The years of education and training for professional practice as a psychologist would be of little benefit to clients unless those skills were presented to the public. Licensure can be considered as a bridge smoothly connecting professional training with professional practice.

STRATEGY

Licensure candidates need to:

- use the metaphor of the bar examination in law or the parallel of medical licensing to philosophically understand licensing;
- conceptualize preparation for licensure as one ingredient in an overall continuing education career development plan;
- be realistic about licensure, be reflective about training and preparation, and think ahead to the future;
- be reflective but not lose momentum.

TIME FOR FINAL ANALYSIS

In the preceding pages, a systematic overview of preparatory strategies for the Examination for Professional Practice in Psychology (EPPP) was discussed and reference was made to several preparatory study designs that may help organize the learning and study process for licensure candidates. Most candidates already know much about learning and information processing. In fact, some candidates for licensure possess exacting knowledge of precise studies, detailing learning, memory, and cognition. Taken globally, candidates demonstrate a high level of cognitive prowess, physical endurance, and intellectual acumen. Their attainment of a doctoral degree in psychology exemplifies these qualities.

However, a doctoral degree does not guarantee licensure. Notwithstanding their high level of intellectual ability and academic training, the vast majority of candidates for licensure still possess some degree of apprehension. Fortunately, apprehension can motivate candidates to properly study and prepare for the EPPP. Unfortunately, each year, a number of highly qualified, bright, intelligent candidates do not pass the examination. Of course, similar truisms could be said of medical school students preparing for medical boards or law school graduates preparing for the state bar examination. Among the professions that require licensure for professional practice, there are candidates who do not pass the requisite examinations for practice without careful study.

Although for many years it was not necessary for psychologists to obtain licensure, today licensing standards in force throughout the United States increasingly make licensure a key credential for all who are interested in offering psychological services to the public.

If certain candidates can disregard preparatory study but still pass the licensure examination, so much the better. Some people possess adequate knowledge to acquire licensure without preparation after graduate or professional school. Others are not so lucky.

Many candidates will find it necessary to devote a significant amount of time to study and preparation for the licensing examination. However, careful study should not be viewed as a sign of personal weakness, nor as an indication of poor or inferior training. Far from it. Some university programs do not teach the specific points or issues that the licensure examination may assess. Or they may teach or emphasize other issues not directly tested on the examination. Also, the mission of doctoral degree programs is larger than solely preparing graduates for licensure, just as medical schools have a mission that goes beyond training graduates who will simply pass their various examinations for practice. Licensing does not assess all components of training.

Putting aside the ideological reasons why professional schools of psychology and university training programs may or may not, should or should not, or can and do not teach and graduate students who all successfully complete licensure requirements, there are sound reasons to carefully prepare and study for the EPPP.

IMPEDIMENTS AND ROADBLOCKS

What happens when a candidate with a Ph.D. in clinical psychology from a program lacking regional accreditation makes application to the EPPP? What happens when a Ph.D. in school psychology from an American Psychological Association (APA) approved program makes application for licensure with a predoctoral internship that lacks face-to-face supervision and involves supervision from a licensed marriage and family therapist rather than a psychologist? What do the ethical standards say about such questions?

You may need to know answers to these kinds of questions. First, you should know the answers because questions involving ethical dilemmas can be included on the examination. Second, you may need to know these and related preparatory issues in order to adequately assess your own preparation for licensure.

Licensure boards for psychologists set specific eligibility standards for the EPPP. Candidates must possess certain credentials and adequate knowledge to pass the licensing examination at a specific level determined by the state. That means you need to know whether you qualify for licensure, and you need to be sure you possess adequate knowledge to pass the examination.

There is a smorgasbord of study strategies that can enhance your efforts to prepare for the licensure examination. Practice examinations involving multiple-choice questions and

Self-Assessment Exercise 7-1

How much preparation have you accomplished so far?

_____

_____

_____

_____

Have you taken a practice examination?

_____

How many of the strategies discussed in this text have you implemented?

_____

_____

_____

_____

Do you have a study plan? What is it?

_____

_____

_____

_____

Self-Assessment Exercise 7-2

What do the regulatory standards in your state require for licensure?

_____

_____

_____

_____

_____

Do you meet the standards?

_____

Do you know the APA ethical standards?

_____

_____

_____

Do you know if an individual can become a licensed psychologist with a doctoral degree in clinical, counseling, or school psychology from a program lacking regional accreditation?

_____

_____

_____

_____

Self-Assessment Exercise 7-3

Conduct a self-assessment regarding how you feel about preparing for the licensing examination. Are your feelings enhancing or hindering your study efforts?

_____

_____

If your feelings interfere, examine how you might address this issue. How can you balance your feelings about licensure with your desire to acquire licensure?

_____

_____

_____

explanatory answers are one obvious learning tool. But many more strategies also have been reviewed, including the need for proper rest and nutrition and the need for secure identified study periods. Is licensure important to you? Study can help.

LOOKING BEYOND LICENSURE

It is also important to look beyond licensure. By necessity, this book largely focuses on the training requirements leading to the goal of becoming a licensed psychologist. However, there is life after licensure. Above all, this is one of the very reasons why licensure should be attained.

In a real sense, readers should realize that psychology is a doctoral profession. Consequently, licensure for a doctoral practitioner is undeniably attractive. It must be noted, however, that many mental health specialties do not require similar education and training. Many professionals advocate education and training for professional practice for those with a master's degree.

In general, although subdoctoral practitioners offer important contributions—just as nurses and physician assistants serve a critical role in the medical field—the doctoral degree as a requirement to become a licensed psychologist offers a sense of independence and professional esteem that can be intensely appealing. Unquestionably, the employment options available to psychologists, ranging from independent practice to local hospital positions, are one of the motivations for becoming a licensed psychologist.

These are not all the reasons one becomes a licensed psychologist, however. If you want to become a psychologist, it doesn't matter how similar other professional venues may be, such as marriage and family therapy or clinical social work, nor how wide the employment options of subdoctoral training. If you do not want to become a psychologist and complete a doctorate and licensure, it does not matter, either.

Following licensure, some psychologists may pursue further specialty training. Psychoanalytic psychotherapy and pediatric neuropsychology are two areas in which postdoctoral institute training is not uncommon. One friend and colleague, Melinda A. Hennen, Ph.D., a licensed psychologist in private practice in New Haven, Connecticut, is a superb example of a clinician who pursued further professional training after completing the requirements for licensure. Her professional career is a model of excellence.

As one deeply committed to continually refining and expanding her skills, Dr. Hennen has pursued extensive training since completing her Ph.D. in school psychology from the University of Georgia and the requirements for licensure as a psychologist. Although a gifted clinician with stellar credentials, she has pursued further training involving marital and family therapy, supplementing her training as a licensed psychologist by completing the supervisory and clinical training required for the designation of Clinical Member in the American Association of Marriage and Family Therapy and State of Connecticut certification as a marriage and family therapist.

For her clients, of course, professional credentials mean that Dr. Hennen offers treatment that ascribes to the highest standards of the profession. For our purposes, this illustrates the fact that licensure need not be viewed as an end to training but as one component of an overall professional development plan. Professional training should not end with licensure.

Self-Assessment Exercise 7-4

Consider your long-term career goals and interests. Do you have particular specialty interests?

_____

_____

Do you plan to seek specialty certification or professional designations in such areas as biofeedback, hypnosis, pain management, neuropsychology, or marital and family therapy?

_____

_____

Have you considered further degrees, such as an M.B.A. or M.P.H., as part of an overall plan for a career in administration?

_____

_____

List one or two areas you might consider pursuing further after you become a licensed psychologist.

_____

_____

CONCLUSIONS

Without a doubt, the magnitude and importance of licensure has grown. Obviously, too, there are those who will find fault with the process of examination for licensure. Because licensure is required for independent practice, though, there is a potential advantage to acquiring license credentials. There are also people who may allow strong feelings or beliefs to interfere with proper preparation. Licensure standards are defined in state statutes and clearly delineate who is and who is not eligible and what is required for eligibility.

Eligibility requires proper education and training, which can lead to acceptance to take the EPPP. But, it does not guarantee a passing score.

Your immediate task is to develop a workable plan of preparation. Partly this can be accomplished by understanding that licensure can represent a capstone to years of education and professional training. Partly, too, it can be accomplished by understanding that licensure can unveil new professional opportunities. Because of this, the following chapter contains examples of professional portfolios (i.e., cover letters and resumes) for those who see licensure as a requisite credential for securing new professional positions.

The critical issue for students and for candidates, remains how to most effectively complete the examination process. The answer is less complex than one might imagine. There is no alternative except to prepare systematically for examination.

In reflectively considering licensure, you should:

1. Use the metaphor of the bar examination for lawyers or medical boards for physicians to understand licensure.
2. Conceptualize preparation as part of a continuing education career development plan.
3. Be realistic and don't interpret the need for long-term study as a sign of weakness.
4. Identify impediments and roadblocks.
5. Review state regulatory standards.
6. Conduct a self-assessment.
7. Avoid falling victim to inertia.
8. Look toward licensure.
9. Look beyond licensure.
10. Consider long-term career goals.

My objective for this book has been to provide a review of key issues related to application, preparation, and licensure. Ask yourself what importance licensure has for your professional goals. How and when are you going to prepare? Have you begun your preparatory program?

8 Designing a Professional Resume

Chapter Preview

HOW CAN I PREPARE MY RESUME AND COVER LETTER?

PURPOSE

There are an ample number of published books containing sample resumes. However, examples of professional resumes for newly licensed psychologists are less than plentiful.

STRATEGY

A professional resume for a licensed psychologist can include:

- critical information on educational attainment;
- highlights of predoctoral and postdoctoral training;
- licensure status and professional designations;
- professional skills and competencies.

FUTURE CONSIDERATIONS

Many emerging (and established) psychologists find it necessary to assemble a professional portfolio, whether they are graduate students completing predoctoral training, postdoctoral residents preparing for licensure, or newly licensed psychologists pursuing a professional position. Generally, this means developing a resume and a cover letter. But, as most psychologists quickly learn, most resume instruction books do not address the specialty training and background required of licensed psychologists. That did not matter, of course, when there was a shortage of psychologists.

Today, however, a comprehensive professional resume, reflecting professional training, clinical skills, and specialty licenses and/or certifications is often a necessity even to qualify for an interview. In addition, psychologists pursuing consulting contracts, medical school appointments, or hospital positions are often requested to provide an up-to-date resume. Commonly, those who pursue university positions will refer to it as a curriculum vitae rather than a resume, a more detailed and comprehensive document than is typically discussed in most resume guides. For our purposes, the examples provided in this chapter could appropriately be described by either term, although certainly those who choose to craft a detailed curriculum vitae would add a complete listing of accomplishments that might include professional presentations, examples of grant writing, and a listing of publications. In any event, a professional resume or curriculum vitae is a common necessity for psychologists interested in pursuing new employment options.

If you are a new Psy.D., Ph.D., or Ed.D. who moved directly from an undergraduate program to graduate school, you probably have accrued a large amount of experience. Due to the rigor of licensing standards, many clinicians completing licensing requirements have completed a number of practica, fieldwork, and clerkship experiences, in addition to their internship training.

As an example of the excellent clinical training one can accrue while pursuing a doctoral degree, at the California School of Professional Psychology (CSPP), the clinical psychology students typically accrue between 8 and 40 hours of experience each year. Consequently, by the time the Ph.D. and Psy.D. students complete their predoctoral internships (CSPP awards both the Ph.D. and Psy.D. degrees), some candidates may have accrued experiences in community mental health clinics, psychiatric inpatient units, university counseling centers, diagnostic facilities, AIDS prevention programs, or any number of mental health placements.

Many psychology students amass considerable clinical experience. Of course, the depth and variety of experiences can vary markedly from one person to the next. Likewise, program specifications also vary from university to university and from one professional school to another, and this can have a marked influence on the experiences of the graduates. Because of such differences, four examples of professional portfolios are presented in Appendix 8A at the end of this chapter. Although the issues in the portfolios are real, the names, facilities, and addresses are fictitious. The people described reflect combinations of experiences not uncharacteristic of psychologists. I have tried to provide four portfolios that can serve as working guides for readers interested in developing or refining their own resumes. In addition, a resume worksheet and checklist of professional skills that you can use to develop your own resume are included in Appendix 8A, following the sample portfolios.

COVER LETTERS AND RESUMES

Developing a resume can be a most rigorous and frustrating chore for many people. After all, a resume presents an initial impression to a prospective employer and any mistakes can present an appearance less than ideal.

Because of my deep conviction of the importance of careful documentation, I have endeavored to present four portfolios in Appendix 8A that address themes that many aspiring or newly licensed psychologists may encounter. The examples range from a person beginning a second career to a recent graduate entering the job market for the first time.

The combinations of areas of practice and experiences were selected to enhance authenticity and to maximize the utility of the sample portfolios for readers. Names of universities and cities were created so as not to lend importance to any one actual institution over another. Readers should see these as illustrative examples included simply to help provide a starting point. Toward that end, a number of worksheets designed for psychologists beginning to construct their resumes are also included. As with the licensure examination, candidates must provide the information to make their own backgrounds come alive. Otherwise, rigor mortis will set in. Consider each sample in Appendix 8A carefully.

CONCLUSIONS

Whether you are a Ph.D. or Ed.D. in clinical, counseling, or school psychology looking for an entry position following a post-doctoral residency, or a seasoned veteran freshly armed with a Psy.D. and looking for a medical school appointment or a new consulting contract, a professionally prepared cover letter and resume are critical employment tools. Unfortunately, most resume books do not address the specialty training and background required of a licensed psychologist.

Fortunately, most clinicians preparing to become licensed psychologists have amassed an impressive array of professional skills and clinical training experiences. In point of fact, many doctoral students who are completing training at one of the many professional schools of psychology complete several clinical placements and training appointments even prior to completing their psychology internship. Similarly, many students emerging from university programs possess fine clinical training experiences, in addition to having completed rigorous research experiences that would augur well on a resume or curriculum vitae.

Unfortunately, many candidates preparing to become a licensed psychologist do not feel comfortable organizing and presenting their background training and skills. But, to ignore (that is, omit) key training experiences and past accomplishments is to minimize the likelihood of successfully securing a professional appointment. Therefore, candidates would do well to prepare carefully a professional resume or curriculum vitae that reflects their past accomplishments.

Although there are unique differences between a candidate who enters a doctoral program after working for several years in a management or health care position and a candidate who enters a doctoral program fresh from an undergraduate baccalaureate degree program, no candidate can qualify to become a licensed psychologist without completing an impressive array of training experiences. The professional resume should:

1. Highlight predoctoral and postdoctoral training.
2. Showcase practicum, fieldwork, clerkship, and internship training.
3. Provide a detailed accounting of accomplishments.
4. Showcase licensure status and professional designations.
5. Emphasize professional skills and competencies.

Naturally, different individuals will want to emphasize different background experiences. A candidate who has served for several years as a certified marital and family therapist in a child guidance clinic, or a candidate who has presented papers at regional and national conferences, will want to highlight those accomplishments. The fact is, candidates need to reflect those individual strengths that best portray their individual backgrounds and training experiences.

You should consider carefully the sample resumes included in this chapter. Recognize the differences between each sample resume. Evaluate your background and develop a professional portfolio that reflects your best strengths.

APPENDIX 8A

Sample Portfolio 1

Sample Professional Resume and Cover Letter

Recent Graduate
Specialty Licensure

PAMELA H. DOE
Ph.D., Clinical Psychology
Southeastern School of Professional Psychology
Child Clinical Psychologist

Highlights:

APA Doctoral Degree
Specialty Training in Marriage and Family Therapy

21 Pleasant Drive
Southern City, LA 64703
Tel: 592-243-5101

September 1, 1994

Marvin Durbin, M.D., F.A.P.A.
Clinical Director
University Medical Hospital
Rock Bluff, AR 74328

Dear Dr. Durbin:

Please accept this letter as formal indication of my interest in your opening for a Child Clinical Psychologist.

As you will note from my enclosed resume, I am presently completing a post-doctoral fellowship at Children's Hospital in Southern City. During my tenure on the pediatric unit I have been involved in weekly hospital staffings, have completed comprehensive diagnostic evaluations on a diverse caseload, and have maintained an active involvement in individual, group, and family therapy.

What may not be apparent from my training is my sincere interest in this position. The University Medical Hospital's experience and reputation for working with young children is of national scope and would be an ideal match to my interests and background in child clinical psychology. Moreover, I am extremely attracted to this opening.

Naturally, I hope you shall find the enclosed information of assistance in your screening. Should you require additional background material, or if you have an interest in seeing a sample diagnostic work-up in order to better assess my skills as a diagnostician in the child clinical area, please do not hesitate to contact me. I would be delighted to forward any supplemental information you would like to see.

I shall look forward to hearing from your office.

Sincerely,

Pamela H. Doe, Ph.D.
Child Clinical Psychologist

PAMELA H. DOE

21 Pleasant Drive
Southern City, LA 64703

Objective:

A challenging appointment on a pediatric unit affording opportunities to contribute professional interests blending child clinical psychology and family treatment.

Education:

Ph.D., Southeastern School of Professional Psychology
    Major: Clinical Psychology, 1992

M.A., Middle Valley State University
    Major: Marriage and Family Therapy, 1987

B.A., Middle Valley State University
    Major: Psychology, 1985

Licensure:

Louisiana State Board of Examiners of Psychologists
    Licensed Psychologist, License #1475

Professional Experience:

Postdoctoral Fellow, Department of Child Psychology
Children's Hospital, Southern City, LA, 1992 to Present

Serve as postdoctoral fellow on pediatric inpatient unit. Provide individual, group, and family therapy, conduct psychological evaluations, and receive weekly individual and group supervision.

Psychology Intern, Department of Psychiatry
Riverview Medical Center, Southern City, LA, 1990-1991

Provided comprehensive psychological services to inpatient residents on drug and alcohol unit and to outpatient population. Major accomplishments:

- completed program evaluation study on length of stay;
- served on local advisory task force on drug abuse;
- served as co-therapist for weekly group therapy.

PAMELA H. DOE — p. 2

Professional Experience (Cont'd.):

Marital and Family Therapist
Valley Family Center, Middle Valley, AR, 1987-1988

Provided individual, couples, and family therapy to regional population. Maintained caseload of 15 families, orchestrated weekly parent education meetings, and served on community taskforce researching behavior disorders in local adolescents.

Marital and Family Therapy Intern
Valley Child Guidance, Middle Valley, AR, 1985-1987

Provided individual and family therapy to children and families. Maintained caseload, participated in case conferences, and received weekly individual and group supervision from agency and university supervisors.

Professional Affiliations:

Louisiana Psychological Association
American Psychological Association
American Association of Marriage and Family Therapy

References:

Available upon request

Sample Portfolio 2

Sample Professional Resume and Cover Letter

Second Career Graduate

PAUL SYDNEY DAVIDSON
Psy.D., Downstate University, Hopeville, CT
M.B.A., City University
Licensed Psychologist/Administrator

Highlights:

Second Career Experiences
M.B.A. and Administrative Background

4 Courtyard Row
Hopeville, CT 37601

June 1, 1994

Elizabeth J. Rowe, Ph.D., A.B.P.P.
Director
Midstate Hospital
Centralia, NY 89125

Dear Dr. Rowe:

Choosing a new administrator, particularly a clinical director, can be a challenging task. Most likely you will see many resumes. Some will capture your interest. Others won't.

I think my background is worthy of consideration.

As you will note from my resume, in addition to my training in professional psychology, I have a strong background as an administrator, having spent ten years working as part of the management team in the insurance industry. Beyond this experience, though, I also possess the managerial training that typifies an M.B.A. This background, in conjunction with the training and expertise that I have acquired while earning my doctoral degree, and my credentials as a psychologist offer a strong mix that would serve your program well.

My clinical interests include projective theory, cognitive developmental therapy, and group process. My administrative interests involve quality assurance, program evaluation designs, and supervisory consultation models.

I would welcome the opportunity to meet with you to explore this position. In the meantime, please do not hesitate to contact me if I can provide any additional information.

I hope we shall have the opportunity to talk soon.

Sincerely,

Paul S. Davidson, Psy.D., M.B.A.

PAUL SYDNEY DAVIDSON

4 Courtyard Row
Hopeville, CT 37601

EDUCATION

Doctor of Psychology

Downstate University, Hopeville, CT, 1990
    Major: School Psychology
    Specialty interests: Child and Family Treatment

Master of Business Administration

City University, Capital City, MA, 1975
    Specialty: General Management

Bachelor of Science

Mill Valley College, Mill Valley, CT, 1973
    Major: Elementary Education

LICENSURE AND CERTIFICATIONS

Connecticut Department of Public Health and Addiction Services
    Licensed Psychologist, License #2825

National School Psychology Certification Board
    Nationally Certified School Psychologist #1664

CLINICAL EXPERIENCE

Clinical Director
Child Guidance Clinic, Hopeville, CT, 1990 to present

Responsible for administration and supervision of comprehensive child guidance clinic providing individual, group, and family therapy and comprehensive assessment services. Clinical staff include two social workers (M.S.W.), one part-time psychiatrist, and one part-time psychologist (Ph.D.).

PAUL SYDNEY DAVIDSON — p. 2

CLINICAL EXPERIENCE (Cont'd)

Child Psychology Resident
Valley Children's Hospital, Hopeville, CT, 1989-1990

> Provided psychological services to clinical and educational treatment program. Responsible for oncall clinical case coverage. Maintained clinical case load. Served as liaison to agencies and schools.

School Psychology Intern
Highview Elementary School, Mayville, CT, 1988-1989

> Provided comprehensive psychological services during graduate internship. Provided individual and group therapy, participated in multidisciplinary staff meetings, and provided teacher and administrator consultation.

ADMINISTRATIVE EXPERIENCE

Assistant Director, Employee Benefits Division
Claim-Free Insurance Inc., Mason Springs, MA, 1980-1985

> Provided administrative support services for national insurance group. Coordinated employee assistance program, managed contractual consultive services, and served as office manager for employee health services center.

Coordinator, Center for Continuing Education
Claim-Free Insurance Inc., Mason Springs, MA, 1975-1980

> Coordinated training for five state-wide insurance corporations using Claim-Free's training facilities. Responsible for management of office staff, consulting teams, and budget. Recruited while completing M.B.A. program.

PROFESSIONAL AFFILIATIONS

Connecticut Psychological Association
American Psychological Association
National Association of School Psychologists

REFERENCES

Available upon request.

Sample Portfolio 3

Sample Professional Resume and Cover Letter

Consultant/Counselor

ELIZABETH D. DAMON
Ed.D., Counseling Psychology
Eastern University

Highlights:

Identified Professional Competencies

Elizabeth D. Damon, Ed.D.
Licensed Psychologist

310 Spruce Hollow
Central City, WI 53726

December 1, 1994

James L. Butler
Director of Human Resources
Zephal World Wide
Longview, OH 41037

Dear Mr. Butler:

As follow-up to our telephone conversation, I have enclosed a copy of my professional resume and a sample one-page overview of selected topics that might be of interest to your division.

Damon Consulting can bring a strong background in organizational development and human resources counseling to your corporation. In the past, I have been involved in varied challenges, from analyzing group dynamics, to redesigning performance appraisal systems, to leading workshops on stress reduction and motivation. Naturally, if you are interested I can forward feedback and evaluation data.

Certainly, employee feedback is always one of the most critical variables that must be assessed when considering consultant services, and I think you might be pleasantly surprised to see the comments that participants have offered.

Should you find the enclosed material of interest, and if you have an interest in having Damon Consulting design an inservice program tailored to your corporations's needs, please do not hesitate to call. I have an impressive consulting team of human resources specialists—professionals with loads of practical experience, equipped with the requisite intellectual and professional skills to design stellar workshop presentations for your company.

Frankly, we hope you will give us a call.

Sincerely,

Elizabeth D. Damon, Ed.D.

Proposal

Training and Development Series

Audience

**Administrative Management
Human Resources Personnel
Employee Assistance Counselors**

Presenter

**ELIZABETH D. DAMON
Ed.D., Eastern University
Licensed Psychologist
Human Resources Counselor and Consultant**

Selected Training Opportunities

**Handling the Difficult Employee
Resolving Labor-Management Disputes
Negotiation Strategies
Interviewing Models
Leadership Models
Motivational Enhancements
Leadership in the Workplace**

ELIZABETH D. DAMON

310 Spruce Hollow
Central City, WI 83726

Objective:

A challenging consulting engagement with opportunities to contribute expertise on counseling/psychology, motivation enhancements, human resources development, and performance appraisals.

Education:

1987-1991
Ed.D., Eastern University
Major: Counseling Psychology

1985-1987
M.A., Willow State University
Major: Counseling Psychology

1982-1986
B.A., Southern University
Major: Psychology. Minor: Business

Licensure:

Wisconsin Psychology Examining Board
Licensed Psychologist, License #3253

Consulting Skills:

Personnel Psychology	Counseling Psychology
Selection & Placement	Interviewing Models
Simulation & Training	Employee Assistance
Leadership Training	Group Process
Work Motivation	Group Dynamics
Performance Appraisal	Vocational Psychology
Stress Management	Management Training

Professional Experience:

1992-Present
Principal
Damon Consulting, Inc., Central City, WI
Provide contractual consultation and counseling services to organizational clients. Selected activities have included employee assessment, staff training and stress management, and employee assistance.

ELIZABETH D. DAMON — p. 2

Professional Experience (Cont'd):

1991-1992

Personnel Psychologist
Lifeline Hospital, Forestdale, WI
Served as Personnel Psychologist
Professional accomplishments include:

- construction of personality measures
- validation of employment appraisal
- inservice training and development
- employee assistance counseling.

University Teaching:

1992-Present

Assistant Professor, Counseling Psychology
City College, Central City, WI
Responsible for teaching M.A. and Ph.D. students in counseling psychology program. Assignments included:

- group dynamics
- group processes in counseling
- counseling: theory and practice
- consultation skills.

Summer 1990

Visiting Lecturer, School of Education
Wayward College, Wayward, WI
Served as adjunct faculty in School of Education counseling psychology program. Teaching duties included:

- human resources counseling
- consulting skills.

Presentations: (selected)

"Consultation Models for Staff Training." 1991. Central City, WI.
"Intervention Strategies for Difficult Employees." 1991. Midvale, WI.

Affiliations:

American Psychological Association
American Psychological Society
American Association for Counseling and Development

References:

Available upon request

Sample Portfolio 4

Sample Professional Resume and Cover Letter

Clinical Psychologist
Minimal Experience

Susan B. Reese
Ph.D., Clinical Psychology
State University of the South
Clinical Psychologist

Highlights:

Practicum Supervisor
Family Violence Expertise

Susan B. Reese, Ph.D.

456 Cliffside Drive
Pacific City, OR 32501
Tel: 983-786-5000 (O)
Tel: 983-782-1779 (H)

John J. Smith, M.D., F.A.P.A.
Clinical Director
Central Shore Medical Center
Ocean Drive, CA 37902

Dear Dr. Smith:

Please accept this packet as a formal indication of my interest in making application for your staff opening for a Clinical Psychologist.

It may be helpful to know that in addition to having received the general training experiences typical for a clinical psychologist, I also possess clinical experience involving assessment and treatment of family violence, psychology of women, and psychosocial epidemiology. I mention this because, given the community focus of your facility, these skills may be of special interest.

Obviously, no slim resume can provide a complete sense of one's professional interests or skills. I know this. You know this, too. As you will see, I have tried to capture something of my professional background. What you won't see is my deep interest in this position. It is, simply put, quite sincere.

I hope we shall have an opportunity to meet and discuss this opening in the near future.

Sincerely,

Susan B. Reese, Ph.D.

Susan B. Reese, Ph.D.

456 Cliffside Drive
Pacific City, OR 32501
Tel: 983-786-5000 (O)
Tel: 983-782-1779 (H)

PROFILE:

Diverse clinical experience involving clinical assessment and treatment of family violence, psychology of women, and psychosocial epidemiology. Specialized expertise:

- **Psychological Examinations:** Provided comprehensive psychological examinations for children and adults, including personality, cognitive, vocational, and behavioral assessment.
- **Practicum Supervision:** Provided clinical supervision to psychology interns completing predoctoral internship training.
- **Clinical Assessment and Treatment of Family Violence:** Provided clinical assessment and court testimony for clinical cases involving violence in the family.

EDUCATION:

Ph.D., Clinical Psychology, 1993
State University of the South

B.A., Psychology, 1988
Classic University

PROFESSIONAL EXPERIENCE:

Clinical Psychologist, 1994 To Present
Clearview Mental Health Clinic, Clearview, OR
Responsible for individual, group, and family therapy, psychological evaluations, and community outreach.

- Designed and facilitated support group for abused women
- Supervised Ph.D. interns in clinical psychology
- Developed and facilitated AIDS education program
- Responsible for individual and family therapy caseload specializing in abused women.

Susan B. Reese, Ph.D.   **Page 2**

PROFESSIONAL EXPERIENCE (Cont'd):

Clinical Psychology Resident, 1993-1994
Clearview Mental Health Clinic, Clearview, OR
Responsible for individual, group, and family therapy.
Provided psychological evaluations and developed group therapy program involving abused women. Professional highlights:

- Participated in weekly case supervision
- Participated in quality assurance program
- Conducted clinical assessment and treatment with violent families
- Developed AIDS education program.

Clinical Psychology Intern, 1991-1992
Ocean Cliffs Psychiatric Hospital, Ocean Cliffs, CA
Provided individual, group, and family therapy during clinical psychology internship:

- Attended weekly individual supervision
- Attended weekly lectures involving adult psychiatry
- Participated in biweekly case conferences
- Supervised practicum students.

RESEARCH:

Reese, S.B. (1933). The genesis of family violence: The influence of family abuse and violence on women's identity development. (Doctoral dissertation, State University of the South). *Dissertation Abstracts International, XIV,* 13758.

PROFESSIONAL PRESENTATIONS:

"Family violence: New directions for victims." Workshop conducted at the Department of Child and Family Services, Ocean Cliffs, CA, May 1993.

"How family violence affects you." Workshop presented at the Family Violence Institute, High Town, WA, August 1993.

AFFILIATIONS:

American Psychological Association
Oregon Psychological Association
National Association of School Psychologists

REFERENCES:

Available upon request

RESUME WORKSHEET

Address:_____

_____

_____

Phones: _____

_____

Objective: Highlight your critical skills.

_____

_____

_____

_____

_____

_____

_____

Education:

_____

_____

_____

_____

_____

Licensure: List state licensure and specialty certifications

_____

_____

_____

_____

_____

Consulting Skills:

_____

_____

_____

_____

_____

Experience: Give years, positions, locations, duties, and accomplishments.

_____

_____

_____

_____

_____

Presentations: Selected list. (Give complete list for university positions.)

_____

_____

_____

_____

_____

Affiliations: **List national, regional, and state memberships.**

_____

_____

_____

_____

_____

References: Available upon request. (For your convenience, list people you've asked to provide references.)

_____

_____

_____

_____

_____

_____

_____

_____

_____

_____

_____

_____

Resume Skills Checklist

Clinical skills	Check	Supervisory skills	Check
Individual therapy	___	Clinical supervision	___
Group therapy	___	Management consulting	___
Family therapy	___	Quality assurance	___
Multiple family therapy	___	Program evaluation	___
Couples therapy	___	Personnel psychology	___
Sex therapy	___	Program planning	___
Play therapy	___	Grant writing	___
Biofeedback	___	Team building	___
Stress reduction	___	Work motivation theory	___
Hypnosis	___	Conflict resolution	___
Intelligence testing	___	Women In management	___
Personality assessment	___	Reward systems	___
Forensic psychology	___	Attitude assessment	___
Chronic pain management	___	Managerial counseling	___
Family assessment	___	Organization diagnosis	___
Neuropsychology	___	Contract negotiation	___
Clinical interviewing	___	Employee assistance	___
Divorce therapy	___	Job enrichment	___
Police psychology	___	Leadership development	___
_____	___	_____	___
_____	___	_____	___
_____	___	_____	___
_____	___	_____	___
_____	___	_____	___
_____	___	_____	___
_____	___	_____	___

Research skills	Check		Check
Research design	___	_____	___
Statistical analysis	___	_____	___
Program evaluation	___	_____	___
Quantitative analysis	___	_____	___
Qualitative analysis	___	_____	___
Survey research	___	_____	___
Data collection	___	_____	___
Action research	___	_____	___
Ethnographic research	___	_____	___
Test construction	___	_____	___
Specialty skills:			
Stress research	___	_____	___
Child assessment	___	_____	___

9 From Preparation to Examination

Chapter Preview

HOW CAN I MAKE THE PASSAGE FROM PREPARATION TO
EXAMINATION?

PURPOSE

There are many strategies and practice exercises that can be
beneficial in providing a smooth transition from preparation to
examination. Ongoing self-appraisal and practice are keys to
success.

STRATEGY

Mastery of examination concepts can be naturally assessed by:

- aiming for 85% to 95% accuracy on final practice examinations;
- using ongoing review strategies for designated areas of
weakness;
- using notecards to review weaknesses;
- striving toward overlearning.

TARGETING EPPP SUCCESS

The intention of this text has been to assist and support a systematic review process for candidates preparing for examination leading to credentials for licensure. As such, systematic preparatory strategies have been presented to aid candidates.

Overall, candidates for licensure as psychologists must possess considerable psychological information. However, it is not enough just to know theory. You must also be sufficiently familiar with the format of the Examination for Professional Practice in Psychology (EPPP) so that you can decipher sometimes highly complex questions and accurately discriminate between the correct answer and items that may, at first glance, appear plausible. Consequently, carefully designed study strategies designed to help candidates maximize the likelihood of success have been presented.

Self-Assessment Exercise 9-1

Are you familiar with the specific examination requirements in the state in which you intend to practice?

_____

Are you familiar with each content area assessed by the EPPP?

_____

_____

What areas do you expect to be most challenging?

_____

_____

What can you expect specifically on exam day? You can expect the EPPP to include 200 multiple-choice questions. Expect certain questions to be sufficiently difficult that you will not know the correct answer. Expect to experience a degree of frustration, at times, as you select the one correct answer from each of four options. If you have studied and prepared carefully, expect to experience a degree of familiarity with at least a number of questions. Also, you can expect to feel tired after four hours with the EPPP.

FINAL PREPARATIONS

The goal of this preparatory program is to prepare for the licensing examination. However well-prepared you are, the examination will likely provide at least one surprise. Maybe two surprises. Fortunately, though, the EPPP is passable. But passing does require effort. Ideally, candidates enter the examination knowing the test material thoroughly. Cold. Candidates also should know what to expect.

Candidates should know, too, that the EPPP is not the only requirement for licensure. Some states administer additional examinations, including oral or essay exams. Because of this, candidates should investigate carefully the individual state requirements.

Successful candidates know that in addition to investigating specific state requirements, preparation should also include a minimum of two final practice examinations that mirror, as nearly as possible, the actual examination process. Ideally, this will include practice examinations conducted on the same day of the week and at the same time as the examination itself.

Candidates should aim for 85% to 95% accuracy on the practice exams during the EPPP final preparation period. The increased accuracy goal is a critical ingredient of the transition from preparation to examination. In the final days of preparation, candidates should be able to identify and understand why each answer on the practice exams is correct, as well as reasons that individual answers are incorrect.

Disciplined review of incorrect items is critical. After each practice examination, candidates should outline areas of weakness and refine study blocks that specifically target areas for improvement. At this point, notecards and audiotapes can be reviewed at different times of the day to maintain overall knowledge, help in learning critical areas of weakness, and assist in overlearning the material. Fine-tune your study efforts in the last month of preparation.

During the last month of study, try to devote at least one-third to two-thirds of your study time to reviewing the practice examinations. At this point, you should minimize wasted time.

MAINTAINING AN ACTIVE ORIENTATION

In real life and on the EPPP, an active rather than an inactive orientation can maximize success. Candidates should stay intellectually active during the final stages of preparation. For example, actively address your areas of weakness by using your notecards and audiotapes to review critical points.

Self-Assessment Exercise 9-2

Did you keep track of your scores on the practice examinations? Are your scores increasingly better?

_____

Do you feel psychologically confident?

_____

Do you accept the likelihood that, although you may want 90% accuracy, you will assuredly have some items incorrect?

_____

_____

Candidates also should continue with physical exercise in order to keep fresh and rested. Unfortunately, some people become less than active, not only during the weeks of study time but also during the final days of preparation. Passivity can be a mistake.

Candidates should strive toward overlearning, refining performance on each successive practice examination. If your practice examination scores are at 70% accuracy, try to reach 80%. If your practice scores are at 80%, try for 85% accuracy. And, if you are at 90%, try to reach 95% accuracy.

CONCLUSIONS

Let's start with the bad news. Not all candidates pass the licensing examination. That's just part of the real world. The good

Self-Assessment Exercise 9-3

How active is your preparatory program?

_____

Have you studied in an active way?

_____

Have you blended study with rest, relaxation, and physical exercise?

_____

Is your daily routine beneficial?

_____

_____

news is that no one needs to know everything to become a licensed psychologist. In fact, one can successfully achieve licensure in spite of areas of weakness.

Looking at licensure specifically, there is a wide diversity in training and educational background among candidates striving to become licensed psychologists. Broadly speaking, some candidates come from schools and programs that have strong scientific and research training. Others may possess greater clinical training experiences. Although all candidates are required to complete coursework and training that meet state regulatory standards, they will have different academic degrees (such as Ph.D, Ed.D., Psy.D.) from diverse departments and schools. What this means, in a general way, is that no two candidates are the same.

The route to becoming a licensed psychologist, therefore, varies somewhat, although it is similar in some respects for all candidates. Some candidates will need to study different areas than others, which means that candidates should conduct realistic and honest self-appraisals.

Self-Assessment Exercise 9-4

Have you carefully reviewed state regulatory standards?

_____

Do you know each area tested by the licensing examination?

_____

Have you considered the importance of licensure in your career?

_____

Do you plan to devote sufficient effort and time to your study?

_____

Self-Assessment Exercise 9-5

Have you realistically appraised your strengths and weaknesses?

_____

_____

_____

How many mock examinations have you conducted?

_____

Did you review each question you answered correctly as well as incorrectly?

_____

Did you review each answer in order to fully understand each question?

_____

What areas should you study this week? Next week?

_____

_____

_____

_____

When will you take the next practice examination?

_____

Candidates should spur themselves to study what they don't know. If you skimmed this text, consider rereading and practicing the material. The objective of all this work, of course, is to secure licensure. Neglecting study courts failure unless you happen to be one of those individuals who already is sufficiently knowledgeable to secure licensure without preparation. Otherwise, you should design a study program that will bring you success.

In the passage from preparation to examination, you should:

1. Design a complete study program.
2. Commit yourself to licensure.
3. Use mock examinations.
4. Aim toward 85% to 95% accuracy on mock exams.
5. Use notecards to review weaknesses.
6. Use time effectively.
7. Set goals and strive to achieve your goals.
8. Identify both strengths and weaknesses.
9. Maintain a disciplined study effort.
10. Maintain an action orientation and momentum.
11. Plan your study program and work your plan.

The fact that licensure for psychologists has become so important may reflect the growing acceptance of psychology as a key field in health care. That is certainly a positive. At present, though, your task is to achieve success in passing the Examination for Professional Practice in Psychology.

Okay, the route to becoming a licensed psychologist can be rigorous. I know that. You know that, too. The fact is, it takes years to complete the academic and experiential requirements to earn a doctorate in psychology. In addition, the postdoctoral psychology residency required to become a licensed psychologist means that candidates have expended an extraordinary amount of time and effort to become psychologists. No examination can fully assess that preparation.

However, licensure is not designed for the profession. Simply put, it is designed to help protect the public. Sometimes, of course, candidates who are immersed in study for licensure do not remember such details. The ambiguity of mock study questions, the frustration of differing state regulatory standards, and the tension and anxiety of study sometimes leave candidates without a sense of the rationale behind licensure.

Professional psychology is, fundamentally, a key factor in mental health care. Just as physicians undergo rigorous examinations designed to assess minimal standards of competency for practice in the health care field, so, too, psychologists undergo examinations that afford an opportunity to review academic and clinical training for practice. The examination, of course, is only one component in becoming a licensed psychologist.

Today, the practice of psychology is highly complex. Issues of racism and sexism, multicultural issues, and a changing understanding of the dynamics of mental health illness reflect isolated illustrations of areas where psychologists are challenged to enhance and expand their understanding. Simplistically, no single examination can capture all that complexity. Nor can an examination fully capture the fine points of psychological assessment and treatment, or the nuances of qualitative and quantitative research methodology. Clearly, the human sciences are a complex area.

Most likely, examination standards and procedures required to become a licensed psychologist will evolve further in coming years. Already, a number of conferences have explored postdoctoral residency training in psychology. However, at this point, the reader must focus attention on completing the present hurdle.

What single suggestion can be offered? Study. Study. Study.

Appendix

The ability to practice as an autonomous health care professional is strictly regulated. All psychologists who intend to provide direct services to the public must be licensed by the licensing regulatory boards in the states or provinces in which they intend to practice.

Consequently, candidates interested in becoming licensed psychologists would do well to contact the state or provincial regulatory boards for the states or provinces in which they intend to practice. The addresses of state and provincial regulatory boards and pertinent organizations follow.

DIRECTORY OF REVIEW ORGANIZATIONS, PSYCHOLOGY BOARDS, AND U.S. AND CANADIAN LICENSING OFFICES FOR PSYCHOLOGISTS

Review Organizations and Psychology Boards

Academic Review
30 East 60th Street, Suite 1007
New York, NY 10022

Tels: 212-724-6011
 800-225-3444

Association for Advanced Training in the Behavioral Sciences
3390 Duesenberg Drive
Westlake Village, CA 91326

Tel: 800-472-1931

Association of State and Provincial Psychology Boards
P.O. Box 4389
400 South Union Street, Suite 295
Montgomery, AL 36103-4389

Tel: 205-832-4580

State Offices

ALABAMA

Board of Examiners in Psychology
401 Interstate Park Drive
Montgomery, AL 36109

Tel: 205-242-4127

ALASKA

Board of Psychologists & Psychological Associate Examiners
P.O. Box 110806
Juneau, AK 99811-0806

Tel: 907-465-2551

ARIZONA

Board of Psychologist Examiners
1645 West Jefferson, Room 410
Phoenix, AZ 85007

Tel: 602-542-3095

ARKANSAS

Board of Examiners in Psychology
101 East Capital, Suite 415
Little Rock, AR 72201

Tel: 501-682-6167

CALIFORNIA

Board of Psychology
1426 Howe Avenue, Suite 54
Sacramento, CA 95825-3236

Tel: 916-263-2699

COLORADO

Board of Psychologist Examiners
1560 Broadway, Suite 1340
Denver, CO 80202

Tel: 303-894-7766

CONNECTICUT

Psychology Licensure
Department of Health Services
150 Washington Street
Hartford, CT 06106

Tel: 203-566-1039

DELAWARE

Board of Examiners of Psychologists
Margaret O'Neill Building
P.O. Box 1401
Dover, DE 19903

Tel: 302-739-4796

DISTRICT OF COLUMBIA

Board of Psychological Examiners
614 H Street, N.W., Room 910
Washington, DC 20001

Tel: 202-727-7823

FLORIDA

Board of Psychological Examiners
1940 North Monroe Street
Tallahassee, FL 32399-0750

Tel: 904-922-6728

GEORGIA

Board of Examiners of Psychologists
State Examining Board
166 Pryor Street, S.W.
Atlanta, GA 30303

Tel: 404-656-3933

HAWAII

Board of Psychology
P.O. Box 3469
Honolulu, HI 96801

Tel: 808-586-2702

IDAHO

Board of Psychologist Examiners
Bureau of Occupational Licenses
1109 Main Street, Owyhee Plaza, Suite 220
Boise, ID 83702

Tel: 208-334-3233

ILLINOIS

Psychologists Licensing
Department of Professional Regulation
320 West Washington Street, 3rd Floor
Springfield, IL 62786

Tel: 217-785-0872

INDIANA

State Psychology Board
402 West Washington Street, Room 041
Indianapolis, IN 46204

Tel: 317-232-2960

IOWA

Board of Psychology Examiners
Department of Public Health
Lucas State Office Building
Des Moines, IA 50319-0075

Tel: 515-281-4401

KANSAS

Behavioral Sciences Regulatory Board
900 Jackson, Room 651-S
Topeka, KS 66612

Tel: 913-296-3240

KENTUCKY

State Board of Psychology
P.O. Box 456
Frankfort, KY 40602

Tel: 502-564-3296

LOUISIANA

Board of Examiners of Psychologists
11853 Bricksome Avenue, Suite B
Baton Rouge, LA 70816

Tel: 504-293-2238

MAINE

Board of Examiners of Psychologists
State House Station, #35
Augusta, ME 04333

Tel: 207-582-8723

MARYLAND

Board of Examiners of Psychologists
4201 Patterson Ave, 3rd Floor, Room 329
Baltimore, MD 21215-2299

Tel: 410-764-4787

MASSACHUSETTS

Board of Registration of Psychologists
100 Cambridge Street, Room 1513
Boston, MA 02202

Tel: 617-727-9925

MICHIGAN

Board of Psychology
P.O. Box 30018
Lansing, MI 48909

Tel: 517-335-0918

MINNESOTA

Board of Psychology
2700 University Avenue West, Room 101
St. Paul, MN 55114-1095

Tel: 612-642-0587

MISSISSIPPI

Board of Psychological Examiners
812 North President Street
Jackson, MS 39202

Tel: 601-353-8871

MISSOURI

State Committee of Psychologists
P.O. Box 153
Jefferson City, MO 65102-0153

Tel: 314-751-0099

MONTANA

Board of Psychologists
111 North Jackson
Helena, MT 59620

Tel: 406-444-5436

NEBRASKA

Bureau of Examining Board [Psychology]
301 Centennial Mall South
P.O. Box 95007
Lincoln, NE 68509

Tel: 402-471-2115

NEVADA

Board of Psychological Examiners
P.O. Box 2286
Reno, NV 89505-2286

Tel: 702-688-1268

NEW HAMPSHIRE

Board of Examiners of Psychology & Mental Health Practice
105 Pleasant Street
Concord, NH 03301

Tel: 603-226-2599

NEW JERSEY

Board of Psychological Examiners
P.O. Box 45017
Newark, NJ 07101

Tel: 201-504-6470

NEW MEXICO

Board of Psychologist Examiners
P.O. Box 25101
Santa Fe, NM 87504

Tel: 505-827-7163

NEW YORK

Board for Psychology
Cultural Education Center, Room 3041
Albany, NY 12230

Tel: 518-474-3866

NORTH CAROLINA

State Board of Examiners of Psychologists
University Hall
Appalachian State University
Boone, NC 28608

Tel: 704-262-2258

NORTH DAKOTA

Board of Psychologist Examiners
1406 2nd Street, N.W.
Mandan, ND 58554

Tel: 701-663-2321

OHIO

State Board of Psychology
77 South High Street, 18th Floor
Columbus, OH 43266-0321

Tel: 614-466-8808

OKLAHOMA

Board of Examiners of Psychologists
P.O. Box 53551
Oklahoma City, OK 73152

Tel: 405-271-6118

OREGON

Board of Psychologist Examiners
895 Summer Street, N.E.
Salem, OR 97310

Tel: 503-378-4154

PENNSYLVANIA

State Board of Psychology
P.O. Box 2649
Harrisburg, PA 17105-2649

Tel: 717-783-7155

PUERTO RICO

Board of Psychological Examiners
Commonwealth of Puerto Rico
Department of Health
San Juan, PR

RHODE ISLAND

Board of Psychology
Division of Professional Regulation
Cannon Building, Room 104
3 Capitol Hill
Providence, RI 02908-5097

Tel: 401-277-2827

SOUTH CAROLINA

Board of Examiners in Psychology
P.O. Box 11477
Columbia, SC 29211

Tel: 803-253-6313

SOUTH DAKOTA

Board of Examiners of Psychologists
P.O. Box 654
Spearfish, SD 57783-0654

Tel: 605-642-1600

TENNESSEE

Board of Examiners in Psychology
283 Plus Park Boulevard
Nashville, TN 37217

Tel: 615-367-6291

TEXAS

State Board of Examiners of Psychologists
9101 Burnet Road, Suite 212
Austin, TX 78758

Tel: 512-835-2036

UTAH

Psychology Examining Committee
Division of Occupational & Professional Licensing
160 East, 300 South
P.O. Box 45805
Salt Lake City, UT 84145-0805

Tel: 801-530-6628

VERMONT

Board of Psychological Examiners
Office of Professional Regulation
Secretary of State
109 State Street
Montpelier, VT 05609-1106

Tel: 802-828-2373

VIRGINIA

Board of Psychology
Department of Health Regulatory Boards
6606 West Broad Street, 4th Floor
Richmond, VA 23230-1717

Tel: 804-662-9913

WASHINGTON

Examining Board of Psychology
Professional Licensing Division
1300 S.E. Quince Street
P.O. Box 47869
Olympia, WA 98504-7869

Tel: 206-753-3095

WEST VIRGINIA

Board of Examiners of Psychologists
P.O. Box 910
Barrackville, WV 26559

Tel: 304-367-2709

WISCONSIN

Psychology Examining Board
P.O. Box 8935
Madison, WI 53708-8935

Tel: 608-266-0070

WYOMING

Board of Psychology
2301 Central Avenue
Barrett Building, 3rd Floor
Cheyenne, WY 82002

Tel: 307-777-6529

Canadian Offices

ALBERTA

Professional Examination Office
Suite 740
8303-112 Street
Edmonton, AB T6G 1K4

Tel: 403-492-6850

BRITISH COLUMBIA

College of Psychologists of British Columbia
Suite 10
865 West 10th Avenue
Vancouver, BC V5Z 1L7

Tel: 604-877-1454

MANITOBA

Psychological Association of Manitoba
1800-155 Carlton Street
Winnipeg, MB R3C 3H8

Tel: 204-947-3698

NEW BRUNSWICK

College of Psychologists of New Brunswick
749 Charlotte Street
Fredericton, NB E3B 1B0

Tel: 506-459-1994

NORTHWEST TERRITORIES

Registrar of Psychologists
Department of Safety and Public Service
Government of Northwest Territories
Yellowknife, NT X1A 2L9

Tel: 403-920-8058

Nova Scotia

Nova Scotia Board of Examiners in Psychology
Box 27124
Halifax, NS B3H 4M8

Tel: 902-423-2238

Ontario

Board of Examiners in Psychology
Suite 201
1246 Yonge Street
Toronto, ON M4T 1W5

Tel: 416-961-8817

Quebec

Corporation Professionnelle des Psychologues du Quebec
1100 rue Beaumont, Bureau 510
Ville Mont-Royal, PO H3P 3H5

Tel: 514-738-1881

Saskatchewan

Saskatchewan Psychological Association
7 Irvin Crescent
Regina, SK S4R 5L3

Tel: 306-924-0110

Index